MW01287441

NICE GIRLS DON'T WIN

THE DIAL PRESS
NEW YORK

NICE GIRLS DON'T WIN

HOW I BURNED IT ALL DOWN TO CLAIM MY POWER

PARVATI SHALLOW

Names and identifying characteristics of certain people mentioned in this book
have been changed to protect their privacy.

The Dial Press
An imprint and division of Penguin Random House LLC
1745 Broadway, New York, NY 10019
randomhousebooks.com
penguinrandomhouse.com

Copyright © 2025 by Parvati Shallow

THE DIAL PRESS is a registered trademark and the colophon is a trademark of Penguin
Random House LLC.

Library of Congress Cataloging-in-Publication Data
Names: Shallow, Parvati author
Title: Nice girls don't win / Parvati Shallow.
Description: First edition. | New York : The Dial Press, 2025.
Identifiers: LCCN 2025008473 (print) | LCCN 2025008474 (ebook) |
ISBN 9780593730577 hardcover | ISBN 9780593730591 ebook
Subjects: LCSH: Shallow, Parvati | Television personalities—
United States—Biography | Reality television programs—United States |
Survivor (Television program) | LCGFT: Autobiographies
Classification: LCC PN1992.4.S44 A3 2025 (print) | LCC PN1992.4.S44 (ebook) |
DDC 791.4502/8092 [B]—dc23/eng/20250313
LC record available at https://lccn.loc.gov/2025008473
LC ebook record available at https://lccn.loc.gov/2025008474

Printed in the United States of America on acid-free paper

randomhousebooks.com

2 4 6 8 9 7 5 3 1

First Edition

Book design by Susan Turner

The authorized representative in the EU for product safety and compliance is
Penguin Random House Ireland, Morrison Chambers, 32 Nassau Street,
Dublin D02 YH68, Ireland, https://eu-contact.penguin.ie.

For my daughter Ama

Thank you for turning my Titanic *around*

There is something waiting for us at the edge of the woods, and it is our fate to meet it.

—CLARISSA PINKOLA ESTÉS,
Women Who Run with the Wolves

CONTENTS

PART III *REBUILDING*

PROLOGUE

"*Please help me,*" I gasped, tears streaming down my five-year-old face. My arms and legs thrashed against the murky pond water. *I'm drowning.* The adult I'd trusted to keep me safe had thrown me off the dock into the middle of the pond.

Other kids in the ashram where I lived remained on the wooden platform watching the gruesome scene play out, like a documentary film crew.

My head bobbed under, pulled down by the weight of the water. My arms reached up, fighting back. I forced my face upward. A jolt of electricity ran up my spine. Breaking through the surface, the sun blinded me. My eyes turned toward the flesh-colored blur in front of me.

"Help me!" I felt crazed, powerless.

No matter my begging, my pleading, my tiny vulnerability, the man remained unmoved; he was cold, hard, silent, stone. Hearing my cries, he only backed away, remaining always only slightly out of reach. White hot lightning in my legs.

Again I reached. Again he inched away.

This would become familiar territory to me in my intimate and professional relationships as an adult: afraid my vulnerability would be used against me. How could I put my heart in someone's hands and trust they'd keep it safe? I knew instead that I would have to be hard; I would have to be prepared to fight.

Back in the water, I was close enough to make a final desperate grab. I took a big breath, grasping, skin slipping against skin. My tiny body, head under water. Choking.

I needed this man to save me—from my fear, from this feeling. I needed him to take it all away. But he seemed to be enjoying this twisted game.

I surrendered. Went under.

I'm dying.

Suddenly, I was scooped up, lifted out of the water. Safe in his arms. It was a test, and I'd passed.

Big breath in. The world slowed, stopped spinning. My body flooded with sensations of anger, relief—and a swell of delight.

I felt wildly alive. I'd survived.

And I was hooked. The adrenaline, the endorphins, the dopamine—the rush of survival had its own potent and addictive chemistry. It was bigger than anything I'd ever felt before, and I would chase it for years to come.

The message I learned that day was clear: if I pushed myself hard enough—to the point of complete exhaustion and near death—I could come out on the other side. I could survive. And surviving, I was beginning to believe, was the most exciting feeling in the world.

I'd repeat this pattern throughout my life again and again, thrusting my body into the deep end without a life raft. I'd get cast on reality television and become one of the most formidable contestants of all time. Repeated experiences with trust and betrayal, power and vulnerability, loss of innocence and deceit would haunt me, lurking within the recesses of my subconscious. They would also help me win.

Being cast on these shows felt predestined for me. I was really good at surviving. I'd lived through the new age commune of my childhood and my family's escape. In the aftermath, I'd assimilated into a completely different culture and found a way to claim power in my young female body. And then I took that power and made it work for me, for better or worse.

People I'd trust to keep me safe would betray me. I would also at times become the perpetrator, betraying others. I became obsessed with power dynamics, learning to use them in games, crafting for myself a polarizing public persona and a lucrative career. I was the Mistress of Murder. The Duchess of Deception. The Black Widow.

Life would find a way to force me to remember this feeling from my childhood. It lived in my body, and our bodies always remember what our brains block out.

It would take decades of playing out these scenes over and over again in the public arena until I could begin to see them for what they really were. I couldn't understand why I was obsessed with power, craved intensity, and kept creating chaos for myself until I began writing this book. I had pieces of the puzzle, but not the full picture.

This story chronicles my quest to uncover what was buried: the true power lodged deep within me.

PART I

SURVIVING

1

Flight

"*Catch her!*" my mother whispered urgently as she pushed my two-month-old body out of a window to my father, who was waiting for me below.

"Got her!" he whispered back.

My mom dashed inside to grab a few hastily packed belongings before running out in the pitch-black of night to the car where my dad had me buckled into my car seat, engine running for our quick escape from the commune they'd been a part of for the last five years.

My parents had both been young seekers. My mother, twenty-five, and father, thirty, joined the Kashi Ashram—or "the Ranch," as everyone called it—before I was born. As was the mode in the late 1970s, the community was informed by Hindu spirituality, yoga, and mysticism. Perhaps the most unique aspect of the commune was its fierce, almost otherworldly female leader, Ma Jaya Bhagavati. (More on her later.)

Before they joined the Ranch and met each other, my dad was living in New York City, and my mom, thousands of miles away, was living in Berkeley, California. My dad, Mike, was an explorer with sparkly blue eyes, brown moppy hair, a lean, muscular physique that worked well with his shorter stature, and a sharp, sarcastic wit. As soon as he could, he hitchhiked his way out of his quaint hometown of Colebrook, New Hampshire—population two thousand—and landed in the vibrant buzz of New York City for school. He'd also gotten work as an EMT. Dad's a Scorpio and by nature loves diving into the depths of the mysteries of life and death. So, before he even met the Ranch's leader, he'd already forged his way into the inner circle of the yoga and meditation scene in NYC. He told me that he would lose all track of time in his apartment, sometimes meditating for up to seven hours a day and entering trance-like states without the assistance of psychedelic drugs.

My mother, Gale, grew up in a very religious Catholic household. At church every Sunday, she gathered in community and participated in ritual communion—ingesting the symbolic body of Christ, confessing her sins to the priest, and becoming one with the mind of God through call-and-response chanting in Latin. She said the rhythmic, repetitive chanting would induce a sort of hypnotic trance and provided her earliest experiences of a deeper spiritual connection with transcendent one-ness—and she loved it. All was well until her teen years, when the constraints of Catholicism became more apparent and suffocating. At one point, she recalled wanting to join her friends at the Freemason Princess Ball, but the Catholic church forbade her, saying the Masons were against Catholics. When she left Catholicism she noticed a void in her life, and she longed for connection with the mystery and magic of God.

Mom's Irish roots blessed her with mermaid-long dark-brown thick hair, hazel eyes, and a milky complexion. Her widow's peak makes her face look like a heart, befitting a woman who lives to serve. Her kind and giving nature is balanced by a strong critical mind that prevails in high-stakes, life-or-death situations. Not that she stays calm in these moments, but she certainly knows exactly what to do to contain the fire and put it out. She left her own hometown of Alameda, California, at eighteen, and at nineteen years old was working at a drug rehabilitation center in Berkeley, fielding calls and saving young lives with her every waking breath. Her nervous system was wound tight from her turbulent childhood and the intensity of her days at the rehab center, and she desperately needed some relief. Berkeley was then—and still is—a place that draws in great minds who wish to explore the cutting edge of altered states of consciousness. So it makes sense that Ma Jaya Bhagavati prioritized that stop during her big recruiting tour for the Ranch.

When the raven-haired, mysterious guru came along and held her events in their respective cities, my parents went. They said they each had extraordinary mystical experiences in meditation with the Guru and felt called to learn more. The cultural climate of the era supported this kind of seeking. People were disenchanted with the rigid and divisive policies of religious organizations and there was a growing distrust of government institutions. The outrage over the Vietnam War and the "free love" movement of the hippies of the 1960s was fertile ground these spiritual teachers used to grow their communities. The once stable structures people had relied on for decades were crumbling, and they were reaching for anything they could to help them find something to rely on—something to help them make sense of life and have direction for the future.

Born Joyce Green in 1940 into an impoverished Jewish family in Brooklyn, Ma got married and became a housewife in 1956. After having three children she struggled with obesity in her thirties and enrolled in a weight-loss clinic. There she learned some simple breathing exercises for weight loss. After practicing the breathwork at home she claimed to have visions of Jesus Christ.

Ma skyrocketed to fame in the New York City new age scene after sharing her big news: Jesus had visited her and activated her spiritual powers. Ma's best friend, Bina, verified that she'd personally seen Ma's bloody hands with the marks of stigmata. Though only Bina had witnessed the mystical event, word traveled fast that there was a new guru in town. Ma connected with highly regarded spiritual teacher Hilda Charlton, an American transplant from London. Hilda was a dancer who'd studied Eastern mysticism and meditation in India for fifteen years before moving to New York and was teaching what she'd learned to hungry seekers. Her lectures had grown organically from two students in a tiny apartment to thousands, filling churches on the Upper West Side of the city. My dad was one of Hilda's early students. Like my mother, his Catholic upbringing had opened him up to the world of ritual, mysticism, and miracles. But, when the Catholic priests wouldn't allow my teenage father to participate in a high school singing event because it was hosted by Protestants, he bailed. He wanted to be a part of something magical that would help him transcend his little worldly existence, not one that got caught up in petty labels. A religion that wouldn't let him sing with his friends seemed ridiculous, no matter what kind of blissful afterlife they promised.

When my dad found Hilda, he found the transcendence he was looking for. She helped him learn meditation techniques where he'd sit for hours and lose himself in ecstasy. Hilda also shared her knowledge with Ma, the budding spiritual teacher, and introduced her to spiritual seekers in the area. Dad was interested.

Later, Ma said that the well-known—and recently deceased—Hindu guru Neem Karoli Baba had chosen her as his student from the beyond. She said she'd had visions of him and in these visions he was sharing sacred teachings with her. Baba's teachings revolved around the need to release attachment and ego to realize God. He said that "a learned man and a fool are alike as long as there is attachment and ego in the physical body." He advised people that the ultimate freedom in life comes from surrendering to God's will above everything. Ma touted this message when promoting herself to her followers as a guru, the direct link to God. And, in this way, she gathered devotees like moths to a flame. Devotees like my parents.

Ma's teachings blended breath techniques that induced

altered states of consciousness with interfaith philosophy, tantra, and meditation. She had some powerful, time-tested tools and potent charisma. The physical teachings, meditations, breathwork, and yoga she shared had their roots in Kriya yoga, a style of yoga that has produced powerful health benefits and altered states for centuries. In other words, she wasn't just making this stuff up from thin air. But a lot of her lectures and philosophies were emotionally manipulative fabrications based on her need to be seen as special, aimed at gaining power and control.

During her spiritual awakening and rebirth as a teacher, she relinquished her role of housewife, divorced her husband, and engaged in a controversial romantic relationship with another one of Baba's devoted students, Richard Alpert (Ram Dass). Ram Dass was crazy about Ma, and enthusiastically endorsed her as the real deal. Sometime into their relationship, however, Ram Dass became disillusioned by her. He ended the relationship by condemning her powers as fraudulent.

In his 1976 article for *Yoga Journal* titled "Egg on My Beard," Ram Dass claimed that he'd been duped by the female guru. He criticized her teaching style, calling it "disquieting." But by the time the article was published, Ma had already established herself as a powerhouse spiritual teacher. She had satellite ashrams—communal housing under her spiritual guidance and rules—all over the United States.

Cults, ashrams, and new spiritual communities were popping up all over the country as more Americans wanted something to belong to that could help them make meaning from their lives. Entranced, my young parents joined the masses seeking spiritual enlightenment. In 1977, after giving away most of her worldly possessions, my mother boarded a Greyhound bus clutching only two boxes of clothes. She was filled with excitement about her new life as she took the three-day trip from San Francisco to Sebastian, Florida. My father at first just took short trips to the ashram in Florida as he continued his studies in New York, and on one spring break trip there in 1978 he met my mother for the first time.

They'd both been assigned breakfast duty at the ashram and met in the industrial kitchen in the large hall. It was around three A.M. when my dad sleepily sauntered in for his call time. Mom was already there, fingers purple from chopping beets, dark hair shining under the fluorescent lightbulbs. Their eyes met and they smiled at each other. "We had some good laughs while making large bins of blended salad and pitchers of vegetable juice," Dad recalled.

After graduating college in the fall of 1979, Dad tossed his backpack into the car he borrowed from a friend, who conveniently needed someone to get the vehicle to Florida, and made the long drive down from NYC to move to Ma's ashram for good.

Upon arrival, he was greeted by smiling, loving faces—all devotees of the Guru who'd pledged their lives to the principles of the community, a code of ethics that elevated serving the Guru and promoted the elimination of any personal desires and needs in order to surrender to a divine practice (i.e., abandon yourself and you'll be saved). My parents both shared that they felt immediately accepted and held by the love they received from every member of the ashram.

They didn't have the language or understanding back then, but now, when they talk about it, they describe the intensity of the affection, emotion, and adoration they received as "love bombing"—a tactic used by narcissists and con artists (and *Survivor* winners like me) to emotionally manipulate people into becoming dependent upon them. My parents describe the effect of the love bombing as safe and enveloping, like a warm blanket. They felt a sense of belonging that they'd always craved but never really experienced. For people who received little tenderness, love, and affection as children, the experience was intoxicating—they were instantly hooked.

They settled into daily life on the ashram, living in communal housing, doing chores and working for the benefit of the community. My mom was appointed a role in the daycare center and my dad worked alongside the Guru's inner circle. They liked doing chores for the community. It felt good to wake up at three A.M. during the Amrit Vela—the time when the world is quiet and the mind is most open to drop into deep states of meditation. They were accomplishing something. They built self-respect, integrity, and self-reliance from committing to and doing hard things.

To quote my mother, life on the Ranch was "idyllic." Sometimes they'd be in the industrial kitchen making vegetarian meals, or attending lectures with the Guru, or meditating, or practicing tae kwon do, where they both rose to the ranks of black belt and often toured the area with other members of the Ranch participating in tournaments. Belonging to this group of high-minded spiritual beings, living close to the land and close to God, willing to sacrifice for the greater good and working together toward enlightenment filled a deep void inside their hungry souls. A year after they met, my parents got married. And a little while later, they got pregnant with me.

But then, a few months before my mom gave birth, everything changed. Like a light switch turned off, their world suddenly became very dark.

Once her devotees were locked in, Ma began behaving more erratically. She started asking them to work extra jobs and give all their earnings to her as a show of their spiritual devotion. In return, she offered spiritual protection against generational curses and clearing of past karma. She hooked into feelings of shame, unworthiness, and guilt inside her followers and exploited their desire to be "good." Members of the community, including my parents, were forced to attend all-night meditations, where they might get kicked or slapped by Ma if they gave in to their exhaustion and nodded off. Dad learned how to sleep sitting up. The Guru knew well that the threat of abuse heightened the stress—and thereby the level of compliance—in the room.

Uncertainty surrounding pain and punishment combined with sleep-deprivation and nonstop financial demands created a potent cocktail of chaos and urgency that dis-regulated members so they lost touch with their ability to make healthy decisions. In short, Ma knew that when people are stressed and depleted, they're easier to control.

In the summer of 1982, a few months before I was born,

my parents attended a Ranch party at the house where Ma was living. My father remembers Ma entering the party in an extremely intoxicated state with behavior and movements strikingly similar to someone on a heavy dose of heroin. Her speech was slurred. She had trouble holding her head up and often nodded off. My parents looked at each other in shock. This was the beginning of what came to be known as "the Rampage"—a period of years when Ma's behavior became more erratic, more abusive, and a lot more violent. She insisted this aggressive change was for everyone's highest good; that she was clearing karma in an accelerated way and if people didn't like it then they were weak or unworthy.

During the Rampage, Ma began controlling community members' personal lives. Romantic relationships needed to be sanctioned by Ma or they would be broken up. Once, when Ma got wind that two of her disciples had been sneaking around and dating behind her back, she called the man to her chambers and demanded that he become a celibate monk. He was forced to shave his head and stop seeing his girlfriend indefinitely. He complied.

The only person allowed to create relationships was Ma. She delighted in arranging marriages. On a whim, she'd have her fleet of unwaveringly loyal henchmen call people in the middle of the night, waking them up and changing their lives with one sentence. "You're getting married tonight," they'd say. They would then be ordered to appear immediately in Ma's chambers, a room decorated with paintings she made— different sized stretched canvases of splashy self-portraits, Hindu deities, and Lord Shiva. There she'd perform the marriage ceremony and without further ado, Ma then commanded that the newlyweds go off and procreate. She wanted more: more money. More obedience. More people devoted to her. Sometimes, when these couples delivered their babies, Ma orchestrated elaborate schemes to adopt their newborns, claiming them as her own—called "Ma's kids"—and raising them in communal rooms with multiple adults rotating in and out as parental figures. It's not hard to imagine how much abuse occurred within those walls. Already pregnant with me at the time, my mother was petrified. Would Ma ask for her child?

After my birth, the Guru phoned my parents.

"Name her Parvati," Ma commanded. Parvati was the name of a Hindu goddess and meant "daughter of the mountain." My parents acquiesced to the name, but clutched my tiny body with conviction, unwilling to give me away—and thank God they didn't. I see this as the ultimate act of bravery. Standing up to what they believed was a supreme, terrifying, and all-knowing authority could not have been easy.

My parents brought me home to the communal house where we lived in one bedroom together. It was pure chaos. Families filled the house to overflowing. Closets had been turned into small bedrooms and several families lived in the rooms that were actually built as bedrooms. Some of the garage had also been turned into small, one-person bedrooms. There was a shared living room and a shared fridge. Food items would be labeled with the owners' names but that didn't stop people like my dad's friend Yogi Shavaite from digging his fingers into Dad's peanut butter. When Dad gave him shit about it, he'd just laugh. Mom, who'd just given birth, battled for time in the one shared bathroom.

It didn't take long for the chaos to become unmanageable. On top of the madness of sharing such close quarters with so many people, Ma began forcing people to call their parents and lie to them, saying that they had cancer and needed large sums of money for treatment. Although anyone who left the ashram was vilified—cursed by Ma and harassed by her goon squad—my parents were unwilling to participate in this grandiose deception and hatched a desperate plan to escape.

Which brings us back to the window, and back to my parents' frantic middle-of-the-night escape with baby me.

Catch her!

Terror flooded my parents' veins as they passed their two-month-old between them and out of the window of their room in the overcrowded house. With the hectic activity all around, no one noticed them leave. Driving away from the Ranch, my parents prayed, "Please, Goddess Kali, let no one see our taillights."

Speeding along the dirt path toward the two-lane highway ahead, my parents were officially on the run. Flight survival response activated beautifully and brilliantly to get them out of a dangerous situation. *It worked!* they thought. Some much-needed relief softened their tightly wound chests.

But the relief was short-lived.

Because they left Florida in such a fright, they hadn't set

themselves up with a safe place to land and lick their wounds. After a few pit stops with relatives, they'd ended up at my mom's parents' house in Alameda, California. My mom's sister was escaping an abusive relationship, so she and her two young kids were also bunking there. The madness continued for my parents; they had a newborn, no jobs, no home of their own, and no community or support. They had traded total chaos for the free fall of living without a safety net. Though they knew the place they left was unhealthy, they didn't know what else to do. It wasn't *all* bad, they began to convince themselves. At least they had friends and a community at the Ranch. They had a purpose. They knew what to expect.

Plus, some scary things started happening while we were gone—I came down with pneumonia and landed in the ER; my dad got some weird skin rashes and couldn't find work; my five-year-old cousin contracted childhood leukemia. They thought the Guru's curse might actually be real. During all this, my parents went to see the *Gandhi* movie and my mom was overtaken by the music. "We never should have left!" She wept nostalgically while my dad sat next to her in the theater. Maybe if they made things right with Ma, our family's health would improve, they thought.

And so, my parents decided to go back. They returned to the Ranch four months after they'd hastily left in the dark of night.

This was the stressful environment I lived in day after day. Although I was a baby when the height of it all was happening and too young to have conscious memories of any of it, I wasn't too young to *feel* what was happening around me. Bessel van der Kolk says in his brilliant book *The Body Keeps the Score* that terror and isolation are at the core of trauma and reshape both the brain and body. Because of the way our survival instincts operate, traumatized people experience anxiety, numbing, and intolerable rage. Trauma affects our capacity to concentrate, to remember, to form trusting relationships, and to feel at home in our bodies. My parents had experienced direct abuse by Ma, but as a child, I had only witnessed it happening to others around me at the ashram. Could that be traumatic? As an adult, I relate to all of the symptoms van der Kolk describes, even though *I don't remember* the trauma of my childhood.

As I got older, we never talked about the scary stuff. My parents' coping strategy, like many others, was to ignore the bad and focus on the good. But bad things did happen. And I was there. The imprint of fear lived inside me, and with no clear communication I had no context for it.

As van der Kolk writes, "Exposure to abuse and violence fosters the development of a hyperactive alarm system and molds a body that gets stuck in fight/flight, and freeze." My infant brain may not have had the awareness of being in a traumatic space, but my body would certainly remember.

"Of course you can come back. You're my children," Ma crooned when my parents called. "But I'm afraid I will have to punish you. You've done a very bad thing leaving and I don't want you tainting the others." Then, she used my dad's spiritual name. "Mahad, you will come here right away. You'll live in the dorm and sleep on the floor with the other single men," Ma commanded. She turned her attention to my mother. "Omkar Dasi, you will stay in California with the baby until I say you're allowed to come back."

Mom waited two long, lonely months in Alameda until she finally got the call from Ma that we could return to the Ranch.

"And, when you get here, you are still not allowed to see Mike. You'll be living alone with your baby. I'll tell you when you can see each other again. Maybe never, we'll see," Ma threatened.

Mom was alone with me in their old room at Ganesh house that she had once shared with Dad, without anyone to talk to. The isolation on top of the terror of a near escape and the chaos of coming back almost destroyed her. But my parents, unlike many couples on the Ranch, truly loved each other.

Dad would sneak over at night with packages of diapers and stand in the doorway silently watching me and my mom play together. He cared. That little bit of love was enough to help her survive. Their separation went on for six months—Dad silently watched me take my first steps from his doorway perch. Finally, Ma allowed them to move back into communal housing together. Two years later, my sister, Sodashi, was born.

Life continued, and we settled back into our daily rhythms on the Ranch, together as a family. As strange as it might sound, growing up on a commune was special for me. Despite the difficulties, outside our cramped and crowded living quarters there was freedom and space for me to roam the vast acreage—and there was always a pack of girls for me to run around with, unsupervised. The Ranch was most beautiful when the sun began to set and the light was soft through the trees, casting a magic spell around the community. I'd run to the fire pit where Ma would lead her evening ceremonies. Sometimes people spent hours creating gorgeous designs around the fire with brightly colored rice. I always marveled at their precision and artistry. *It must have taken forever to make those swirls and zigzags.* Knowing the design would be destroyed at the end of the night, I always wanted to take a picture of it. But I didn't have a camera so I drank the beauty of it in, savoring it with my eyes.

As the night grew darker, grown-ups and kids would wander in and seat themselves on the cold concrete around the fire. It was our very own 1980s New Age tribal council, and Ma was Jeff Probst. Maybe there were blankets or cushions strewn about, or maybe people brought their own, knowing how long these nights could last, but my family didn't. I only remember the hard, cold stone under my bony butt. I wiggled around impatiently as the air got thicker and more tense while we waited, not knowing how long it would be until our Rockstar Guru would make her entrance. When she finally did, it was like the opening moment of a Taylor Swift concert. The crowd would rise to its feet, fizzing with excitement. It was time for the Big Show!

Ma swept in theatrically, piles of solid gold bangles clinging together on her wrists as she clapped and chanted. Beautiful bare feet painted with henna jangled with gold anklets wrapped around her lower legs. A metal snake cuff slithered up her biceps. A diamond nose stud adorned her face; it connected to a golden chain linking it to her right earlobe. A red bindi was placed over her third eye. She was a divine being—Kali, the Goddess of Death, the Mother of the Universe. In today's era, Ma—very much a white woman—would probably be canceled for cultural appropriation.

Around the fire, Ma would lead us in hours of chanting, intermixed with lectures on how to live in service and devote yourself to the Guru. I didn't understand anything she was talking about, but I could feel it was important. We were all taking part in confession, and Ma was the priest. People would throw into the fire their "karma," things that had hurt them in the past, sins they'd committed, lies they'd told. Then they would be cleansed. We were mesmerized, hypnotized. All of us synchronized in the rhythm of God. I was a child and I was high as a kite, lost in the bliss of this feeling. One with the universe. Only Love existed.

There were also daytime ceremonies to honor our Guru. On these days, the Great Hall would be bursting with flower arrangements, silks, and a red carpet that ran the length of the room from the doorway up to the Guru's throne. Adorned with flowers, the chair hovered above a bowl of milk and honey and rose petals waiting anxiously to bathe her feet. Bright orange marigolds, the sacred ceremonial flowers of India, lined the carpet on either side. Their fragrance was so sweet and strong it tickled my nose. I watched as fully grown adults—the people who took care of me, the ones who made the rules, the authorities in my little, young life—prostrated themselves, bowed down and kissed the feet of the Guru in a demonstration of devotion to their Higher Power. *This is Love,* I thought.

But even under my veil of childhood innocence, the *not-quite-right-ness* of our lived experience sometimes slipped through. I remember once taking a field trip to the movie theater to watch *The Land Before Time.* I was in first grade at the school they ran at the Ranch and me and my classmates piled into a tour bus to head to the theater. I was pumped, and a little nervous. Group trips off the Ranch were rare. My sweaty palms clutched my brown sack lunch Dad had prepared for the day trip. I sat on the floor of the dark bus next to my friend Ganga. The floor had track lighting, and I could just make out the faces of my friends sitting along the edges of the floor around me. I chewed my cheese sandwich and slugged a swig of Sprite, a special treat. The boy on the other side of me asked for a sip. When I handed him the Sprite he looked at me with disgust. "Ewwww. Backwash!" he yelled, shoving the drink back in my hand. Shame flushed my skin. I was grateful for the absence of light on the bus. When we arrived at our destination, we went wild—elbowing past one another to rush off the bus and score the best seats in the theater. It didn't matter, the teachers assigned our seats once we were inside. We took up two full rows.

I loved the movie. The dinosaurs were so cute, especially Petey the pterodactyl. At some point, I noticed a group of men dressed in all black silently moving through the theater. Then they were gone. The teachers said we had to leave. The movie wasn't finished yet. When we got back to the bus, my friend Ganga was missing. "Where did she go?" I asked. The teachers looked at me, brows furrowed, mouths in a hard line. They said nothing.

Later I'd find out that Ganga's parents had given her to Ma at birth. When they left the commune they'd pleaded with Ma to give them back their baby. When Ma refused, they'd worked with the FBI to organize a sting operation, and a SWAT team had swept into the theater to collect their child.

Over time, my parents worked together to break out of the hypnotic trance from the love-bombing and the cycle of abuse they were trapped in, to tease apart what was real from what was not. While still working in and participating in the community, they slowly started taking steps to build their independence. Like many others, Dad began working outside of the Ranch to make some money. He took a job at a nearby public high school, where he met a therapist who was trained in the teachings of Milton Erickson, a highly regarded hypnotherapist. The man helped Dad to unravel the Ranch indoctrination of indentured servitude and reconnected him to healthier thinking—reestablishing him in his own personal power and authority. With this therapeutic support, my parents made a plan to get us out of the community for good—starting with strategically moving off the Ranch grounds and into a two-bedroom home of our own across the street. They'd told the Guru they'd still participate in community events, but that our family needed more space to live. Because they were valuable, obedient, respected members of the ashram, she'd acquiesced and sanctioned the move.

Once living in their own home, their phone calls were no longer monitored, and my parents had safety and privacy to speak freely. Little by little they reclaimed their voices. They took my sister and me out of the Ranch school and enrolled us in public school. My mom asked Ma for permission to attend community college in Ft. Pierce, Florida. When Ma agreed, Mom became the first person from the Ranch who was allowed to go to college. As my parents' lives became less insular and controlled by tribal dynamics, they met new people outside of the Ranch who were thinking critically and differently. These relationships bolstered their confidence and ability to see another life beyond the Kashi Ashram.

But I wasn't ready to let go so easily. The Ranch was all I knew. It was where my friends and my freedom were. I longed for the Bliss Feeling I found when I was at the ashram. So, I straddled two worlds. I was the girl with the weird name at my public school, learning how to work the system by pleasing my teachers and paying attention in class. I figured out how to make myself popular. I knew blond girls were special because I had Barbies, and so I asked the prettiest blond girl in my class to be my best friend. But at home, all I wanted to do was run back to the Ranch and see my "real friends"—the ones with names like me. The feral ones.

While I was busy learning the system, my mom leaned more and more into her education. She knew it was our ticket out. In addition to her course load, and mothering two small children, she also worked in her school's tutoring lab to help with expenses. She maintained an A average and eventually scored a scholarship to the Florida Institute of Technology. Driving forward with newfound confidence in herself, she applied and got accepted into a competitive master's program in engineering at Georgia Tech. That's when we made the final move away from the Ranch for good. I was nine years old.

The first few months that we lived in Marietta, Georgia, just outside of Atlanta, there were hailstorms, tornadoes, and a blizzard. Were we being punished for leaving Florida by these aggressive acts of God? Maybe. But my parents were pioneers now; we were survivors. And survivors don't have time for fear. My parents devoted themselves to something very different than a magical Guru—they committed themselves to creating a new life for their children.

My dad needed work with a flexible schedule so he could take the lead on the home front. He'd been a sous chef at a French restaurant and a substitute math teacher in Florida and found similar gigs in our new town. My mom worked the graveyard shift at a bookbinding company as she waited for her master's program financial aid to kick in. My sister and I were left to fend for ourselves, to make new friends and learn how to survive in this unfamiliar urban jungle. It was like an iron curtain had dropped, completely severing us from our old life.

It's possible my parents discussed the changes our family was going through with me, but I have no recollection of that. They did tell us that we could change our names if we wanted to, but after compiling a list of mostly Disney princesses, I couldn't settle on anything that fit and stuck with Parvati. I was living in a big, diverse city and I took comfort that the names around me were also unique—my new best friend was a spunky, fun-loving girl named Da-Ewa. Through music, she introduced me to the vibrant youth culture of the 1990s that I'd been missing while living on the ashram. Awestruck, I discovered my new queens—Whitney and Mariah—along with whole new rich, delicious genres of music I'd never experienced on the Ranch, but that touched my soul in the same way the spiritual chanting had. I'm sure losing my old friends and way of life was painful for me, but any sad or lonely memories are blocked out. The vivid ones center around forging ahead. A few of my friends from the commune wrote me letters, but I never replied. Why would I? *I'm never going to see them again anyway,* I thought.

Like my parents, my sister and I had jobs to do. We had to get ourselves to school in the morning. "Come on, Sodash!" I yelled, ripping my backpack off the hook in the front hall and throwing the door open. "We're gonna miss the bus if we don't leave now!"

My seven-year-old sister chased after me, wide-eyed. The school bus was a mythic figure to us that held great power over our day. Our parents were already on their way to work by the time we needed to catch it, so if we missed the bus there was no option B. We sprinted to the entrance of the neighborhood. A wave of relief washed over me as I saw the bus waiting with the door open. *Ahhhh, yes! We made it.*

I slowed my pace.

Just then, the door swung shut and the bus began slowly rolling up the hill.

NOOOOOOOO!

Taking in my little sister's helpless expression, I knew I ·had to lead this charge.

"Run!" I said with fierce determination.

The hill loomed large up ahead, but I knew the bus would stop again at the second entrance of the neighborhood right at the top. Relief was coming, but I'd have to earn it. Together my sister and I sprinted to the top of the hill. We were panting as we stepped onto the bus, and Ms. Anne, our grumpy, short-tempered bus driver, quipped, "Ya'll need to leave earlier next time."

We slid into a couple open seats toward the back of the bus. Ms. Anne liked to yell, so it was better to be far away.

"You kids quiet'n down! Or I'll turn this bus around and ain't none of you goin' to school!" she'd scream at us like a drill sergeant from up front without turning her head. My stomach tightened into a hard ball.

In my neighborhood, all the kids took the bus. All my friends in the apartment complex we lived in were just like us, running around in hand-me-down clothes and eating Kraft Mac and Cheese or frozen fish sticks for dinner. (We'd stopped being vegetarian once we left the Ranch.) My family was poor, but my sister and I never really knew that. I just knew money was a precious resource and that my beleaguered parents worked diligently for it. I wanted to be part of the solution, to help my parents so they didn't have to work so hard. My sister and I sat on the living room floor clipping coupons and watching Saturday-morning cartoons on our TV that sat on a wooden two-by-four propped up on cinder blocks. I made dinner, sometimes forgetting to drain the water out of the noodles, ending up with Mac and Cheese soup. My parents' frugality and determined work ethic paid off quickly. After two years in the apartment, they'd scraped together enough cash for a down payment on an actual house: a four-bedroom behemoth in the suburbs of Marietta with a basement, a garage, a hot tub on the back patio, and a massive fenced-in backyard. We were royals.

A couple years after we'd settled into middle-class suburbia, my little brother, Kaelan, was born. I was twelve, going through puberty, desperate to find a way out of my loner, nerd phase and into a cool group of friends. The baby was cute and cuddly, but he was also loud and messy. My parents were mostly exhausted and snappy. They enlisted my sister and me as babysitters, which I resented with every ounce of my being, but obligation held me hostage. I couldn't let myself be a burden after what my parents had done to save us. I felt an urgent, pressing need to find a way through this new kind of chaos.

It's true that patterns repeat. Many years later, as an adult, I began noticing my own tendency to flee situations that freaked me out (I'd once jetted off to India to avoid breaking up with someone face-to-face): I would gloss over pain, bounce from relationship to relationship, move constantly, often donating everything I owned to Goodwill, and never settle in one place for long. I started delving into my childhood experiences looking for answers to why I did certain things that caused more chaos in my life. At forty, seeking support, I read a book called *Complex PTSD: From Surviving to Thriving*, by Pete Walker. I don't remember how I found this book. The cover looked intimidating, like a college text, but when I dove into its contents, I related on a profound level.

Walker describes trauma types, or four basic survival strategies and defensive styles that develop out of our instinctive fight, flight, freeze, and fawn responses. He says that those who repetitively experience trauma as kids often learn to survive by overusing one or two of these "4F" responses. When I read about the flight type, alarm bells sounded.

Flight types are like machines with the switch stuck "on." They're driven by the unconscious belief that perfection will make them safe and lovable. They rush to achieve. Their minds and bodies are constantly racing to flee their inner pain. This is why Flight types can become addicted to their own adrenaline. They're also susceptible to chronic busyness, workaholism, and can develop stimulating substance addictions.

Well, hot damn. If that didn't sound like me.

2

Fawn

"**S**am Sellars is into you," my friend Becca said to me at lunch between a mouthful of French fries.

"What? Are you serious?" My cheeks flushed. I couldn't believe it. Sam was a football player and just voted most attractive by our whole high school freshman class.

At the beginning of the year, my cool-without-trying blond-haired, blue-eyed BFF, Heather, had encouraged me to join the swim team with her. Heather and I met in the seventh grade when my family moved to our new house in the suburbs, and she was one of my only friends going into high school. I mirrored everything she did. Swim team became a way for me to escape my raucous baby brother and over-worked parents at home and make some more friends. Plus, I needed a new identity—and a new personality—if I was going to survive these next four years.

My days began with high-octane adrenaline. It was fall

and still dark when I dragged my sleepy, heavy body out of bed for early-morning practice. In the pool I was slow, but my flight survival response was strong. It hummed along, keeping me in the water for the full ninety-minute practices. My body was awash with endorphins, exhaustion, and relief when Coach blew the final whistle.

Then I'd rush to the locker rooms and shower quickly to head off to school. Kicking off my days in the pool activated some dormant part of me. I was full of energy and enthusiasm for life. I was happy and friendly. Eventually, my middle school chub melted off my frame and I found a new confidence inside my lean, athletic body. I started getting the good kind of attention from my peers, and for the first time in my life boys were into me.

Though I looked different and acted confident, I still saw myself as the middle school girl I'd left behind just a few months ago: a shy, dweeby theater kid wearing an oversized Tweety Bird T-shirt. Since my recent swim team metamorphosis there was a wide gulf between how the outside world saw me and my own self-perception. Luckily, I found that if I ignored my insecurities and instead beamed my attention on others, I could earn approval and validation. Like many girls, I'd learned how to fawn.

Defined as praising someone too much and giving them a lot of attention that is not sincere in order to get a positive reaction, fawning is a survival strategy that helps people gain approval and fit in with the tribe. It's basically competitive likability.

I thoroughly enjoyed the power that came from being

adored without the vulnerability of liking any of the boys back. It felt like a magic trick to me. I was not remotely interested in a relationship—I had no desire for boys to touch me. My goals were clear: friendship and social status. I wanted to belong to a tribe of kickass girls. The boys were ancillary symbols of our superior female status. I knew that having a few popular, cute guys interested in me at any given time gave me some real clout. I liked them. I just didn't, you know, *like them*. What I didn't realize at the time was that flirtation and friendliness coupled with emotional unavailability and intermittent, icy apathy was a potent aphrodisiac. The boys flocked to me like seagulls at a beach picnic. The competition among them only amplified their interest. Being wanted like this was a high—and I craved more of it.

I had some great and powerful role models for my new incarnation. I was living in the Deep South, where the archetype of the Southern belle was alive and thriving. Stereotypical femininity abounded. Not so much in my own home: Mom was often working overtime at her electrical engineering job. Dad worked as a high school teacher and did most of the caretaking, dinner prep, and chauffeuring me and my sister around, while my wild two-year-old brother refused to put clothes on and spun around like a Tasmanian devil, laughing uproariously. Our house was an anomaly in Southern suburbia. But over at my friends' houses, moms dressed up to run errands—curling their hair, plastering their faces with makeup and false eyelashes, adorning themselves with sparkly baubles and pretty pastel dresses. I wasn't about to go that far, but I noticed the effect these women had on others. Their syrupy sweet accents gave the impression of an innocent baby deer lost in the woods.

"Sahweetie, ahhh need your hehllp," they crooned, batting their thick curtain of eyelashes at whatever man happened to be in their path. The men, in response, were always extra polite, falling over themselves to lend a hand. Watching this as a teenager made a big impression on me. I always knew myself as strong and fiercely independent. At the commune, I was a wild thing running around the South Florida woods barefoot with her band of hell-raisers. But now, in my new life, I wove a little bit of this fawning Southern belle into my persona, playing around with feigned helplessness as a tactic to get what I wanted.

It worked like a charm.

"Buuuut, Mr. P, I worked so hard, and I really believe I deserve an A. I mean, an 89 is so close to a 90, don't you think you could do this one little thing for me and bump it up just one teeeeeny tiiiiny point?" I said to my science teacher. "You'd be a real hero to me, and I would be forever grateful to you." I continued to plead my case in a tiny, raspy voice, leaning in with my hands on his desk.

"All right, but just this one time. And don't tell any of your friends about this. I don't want them coming in here, too," he replied, smiling at me conspiratorially.

There was a current of energy between us. I could feel it. It wasn't that I was interested in sex or anything like that, but there was something charged and electrical in the air around us. "Thank youuuuuu! I'm so grateful. I'm going to get into UGA and be a Pulitzer Prize–winning journalist thanks to you. You're the best," I'd say with a little wink, backing away quickly before he changed his mind. Then, I'd walk down the hall to Mrs. D's room and perform the whole charade all over again. It didn't matter if I was fawning over a man or a woman, for me the strategy was a winner with *all people.*

By sophomore year, my friend Heather started smoking weed and made some new friends who spent most of their time hanging in basements doing drugs and listening to music. I was locked into high-achieving flight hyperdrive and slowing down to smoke weed just wasn't a match for me. I hung out with Heather less and began spending more time with an ambitious group of girls: Paige, Sara, and Becca.

Paige was the class secretary who did everything right. She made straight A's, listened to the Beatles and Elton John, and loved Scarlett O'Hara from *Gone with the Wind.* Paige's parents were strict Italian Catholics—her dad, Arnie, was a prison warden, and her mom, Pam, was a school administrator. Paige was angling for a scholarship to Georgia Tech to study foreign policy.

Sara was a brunette, brown-eyed cheerleader, volleyball player, and weight lifter. She had a goofy laugh that sounded like Mickey Mouse. Just hearing her laugh would crack me up so hard I'd double over crying in the middle of class until the teacher separated us. Sara wanted to be a bodybuilder. One time she misspelled her own name, so we all called her Sas forever after that.

Sas invented a game called Coupons.

"Okay, girls! What do you want?" I shouted over Britney

Spears's music blasting from the passenger seat of Sas's bright orange Ford Tempo.

"Mexican pizza. Diet Coke. Chicken tacos. Cinnamon sticks. Sprite. Nachos!" Paige's and Becca's voices rang out from the backseat. I scribbled furiously on my small notepad, keeping up with their menu items.

"All right! I got it. Let's do this," I said, tearing the sheet out of the notebook, ready for action. Sas confidently repeated our order into the speaker at the Taco Bell drive-through.

"That'll be twenty-two dollars and ninety-three cents," a boy's voice crackled through the speaker.

"Ohhhh, we have a coupon, to get all of that for *free.*" Sas's Southern drawl was unparalleled.

"Huh?" the boy responded, confused.

"We'll explain when we pull up," she said in her sweetest, easiest voice.

The game continued at the drive-through window. We fawned all over this guy like he was Leonardo DiCaprio in *Romeo + Juliet.* The poor little darling was covered in fairy dust and mesmerized by the time he delightedly handed us our complete order without charging us a dime. We ate like kings for four full years playing that game.

Becca was our class president. She was a year older than all of us and drove a car, so we were independent by sophomore year when she turned sixteen. Becca was on the swim team with me. She was also a track star. She ran the eight-hundred-yard dash, consistently placed first, and competed in the state finals. I was also on the track team. I never won, but I gave it all I had. I would run so hard that my legs would go numb, and I'd pee on myself. I'd come in second to last or last place, praying no one could see the pee dripping down my legs through my track shorts.

I played high school like *Survivor*, and I wanted to win. Together, my powerhouse girls' alliance ran the school. We had friends in every group and the teachers loved us. My girls helped me campaign and win a place on student government and homecoming court. As my popularity rose, I set my sights on the coveted Senior Superlatives. There were many categories: Most Attractive, Ms. Sprayberry High School, Most Athletic. By then, fawning was my superpower, and I knew how to play to my strengths—I wanted to win the title of Friendliest. I would cement my place in SHS history with this superlative. I was devoted, playing the long game all year, buzzing around school like a firefly, twinkling at everyone with my megawatt smile. I was always chatting up somebody, always late to class with a wink and a grin. When a new kid moved to school and sat behind me in language arts class, I spun around in my chair to introduce myself. "Hi, I'm Parvati. What's your name?" I asked. In my quest, curiosity was key. If you're trying to make a person feel special, ask questions about them and be deeply interested in hearing the answers. I always asked with a disarming smile and leaned in close for their reply.

Sometimes, my "friendliness" was misinterpreted as romantic interest. I was constantly darting away from boys who thought I wanted to date them. I didn't want to tell them I wasn't interested because then maybe they wouldn't vote for me in the end, and I *needed* their vote. I played coy when they asked me out, putting them off with a little laugh as I walked away. I was called a "tease" and a "prude," labels that I found much more palatable than the alternative "slut" that my girl-friends who hooked up with these boys were called. A "tease" is a woman who is unattainable. A "prude" belongs to no one but herself.

At the end of the year, my hard work paid off. I won my coveted award, a plaque that read, PARVATI SHALLOW "FRIEND-LIEST." I hugged it into my chest, proud of my accomplishment.

At the senior swim banquet, Becca and I stood in a line at the front of the room full of our parents and the other gradu-ating seniors. "What's your big dream for your life?" Coach asked us. Down the row, my teammates answered:

"I want to get a scholarship to Clemson and run track," Becca said.

"I want to go to graphic design school," said Miles.

"I want to move to Atlanta and own my own landscaping business," Corey said.

"I want to move to L.A. and be on TV," I said.

The room erupted with laughter. *What's so funny?* I thought.

In high school I had a little twelve-inch TV with a built-in VHS player in my room, where I watched episodes I'd taped of *Days of Our Lives* and *Buffy the Vampire Slayer*. I thought Sarah Michelle Gellar was flawless, and I wanted to be a strong female lead like her who did my own stunts. In middle school I'd done theater and loved dressing up and receiving applause. Maybe I could give acting a real try. The idea of pretending to be different people and getting paid for it appealed to me.

But my practical engineer mom encouraged me to get a college degree. So I applied to schools in California and New York City, hoping to get a jump on my big-city dreams. In the end, however, I chose to attend the University of Georgia. I had a scholarship that paid for tuition and books. Plus it had a good reputation, and the town of Athens was charming with lots of little local shops and restaurants. I joined a sorority so I could make friends fast and have a ready-made, built-in social life I could count on from the jump.

Rushing a sorority in the South was easy for me. I simply continued the competitive friendship game I'd played in high school. Dressed in my cutest little black skirt and strappy tank, I flirted with the girls in the different houses on the row, giggled at their jokes, and told them what they wanted to hear. "I love your pearls. Where did you get them?" I asked in a soft raspy voice while gently touching their wrists. I scored multiple bids and chose to join AOPi, the sorority that had a gorgeous red-brick house with white columns and the most popular girls from my high school.

Sorority life was full of weird traditions and rules that felt archaic and misogynistic, but I found the girls I vibed with on the fringe, enjoyed the parties, and left the rest alone. "Are you a lesbian?" my mom asked me one day when we were standing in my bedroom at the AOPi house. "Why would you ask me that?" I laughed, a bit offended. I'd prided myself on the collection of boys who loved me and the trail of broken hearts I'd left behind in high school. "Because you have such intense connections and deep friendships with your girlfriends," she explained, a little defensively.

Looking back, I see what she meant. I'd always dated men confidently, but I hadn't ever let myself develop deep emotional connections with them. I was aware that dating and friendship were two different beasts, and it was best to keep them separate. My friendships with girls felt safe. They didn't want to own my body or get something from me that I wasn't sure I wanted to give. They got the true me, while the boys I dated got the performance. Even my friendships with boys felt tinged with sexuality that felt mildly unsafe and kept me from being authentically vulnerable.

With my social life in full swing, I needed cash to pay for all the events, outfits, gowns, and parties. My friend Julea was a waitress at Longhorn Steakhouse and put in a good word for me. Turns out I was born to be a waitress. It was fast-paced and activating, a perfect match for my flight type. No matter that I spilled drinks and forgot orders, I was still the top tip-earner most nights. I never let my customers see me upset. After getting reamed by my manager for messing up orders, I forced back my tears, strode out into the dining room, plastered a smile on my face, paid compliments, begged for forgiveness, and gave a suggestive little wink when I said: "I'll make it right for you."

I carried on like this for four years, throwing myself into bed exhausted after a full day of schoolwork, partying, or waiting tables all night. I was always dead tired, but I felt powerful, satisfied with the cash piling up in my bank account. I spent it on wanderlust: backpacking trips to Europe, spring breaks in Miami, a summer French immersion in Quebec. As college came to a close, I was ready for the ultimate road trip.

"Can I come with you?" my boyfriend Liam cooed. We were standing in my parents' driveway next to my gold Toyota Camry. The car was nearly filled to the gills with blankets, pillows, clothes, and shoes for my big cross-country move. I'd just graduated with a degree in journalism and had secured a very cool job in entertainment PR in Los Angeles. My college sweetheart wanted us to do this next adventure together.

A clear voice rose from my gut. *No, don't come. I want to do this on my own.*

But instead of listening to that voice, I beamed at him and said, "Of course you can come! You can stay with me and my girlfriends until you find a place." *Wait, what? Who said that?* I practically spun around looking for the body that belonged to those words. *Was that* me? What I would come to know as my "fawning voice" sounded hollow and emerged from a superficial place high up in my chest and throat.

By the time I graduated from UGA and my beautiful, green-eyed, Val Kilmer from *Top Gun* look-alike boyfriend was asking to move to L.A. with me, I had taken fawning to an art form. I'd modeled my entire persona on my heroes and the most badass women I knew: Buffy and Britney Spears. They had sex appeal, independence, and I wanted to be them. Buffy, the Chosen One, could defend herself in a fight and protect the innocent. Britney played boldly with her body, voice, and clothes and could command an audience like no one else on earth. They both seemed completely self-possessed and fierce. Aggressive in the hottest way. To me, they exhibited the ultimate power and freedom that came from being invulnerable and independent. Real intimacy terrified me, but I still wanted the validation of being chosen. I knew exactly what to say and how to move my body to make someone feel special and loved, so they would want me, but I always held my guard up. I never let myself get truly soft with anyone, certainly not my own boyfriend. My mode of operating was catnip for men, and I never questioned why I felt the need to act this way. As far as I knew, I was blessed with a gift, and this special power was just part of who I was.

Other people thought my act was the real me, too. When Liam asked to move to Los Angeles with me, he had no clue I'd gone against my instinctive *NO*. He was thrilled I had invited him to stay in my room—which I very much wanted for myself. He *felt loved*. But inside my body, it was like a slumbering anaconda sensed danger from deep within me and slithered awake, tightening around my belly, disconnecting my brain from my vocal cords, constricting my throat, strangling my truth, and replacing it with words of appeasement. Brain fog and muscular tension felt familiar to me, comfortable in their discomfort. This wasn't the first or the last time I'd lie to myself and someone else to avoid conflict.

If I'd had the courage and the awareness to be honest with Liam, I would have told him that I wanted a grand Oregon Trail–inspired adventure. That I thought I'd have a lot more fun if I was single. But instead of saying something I knew might hurt him, I froze my truth deep inside and catatonically watched my gorgeous, kind, perfect boyfriend finish packing me and my belongings into my Toyota Camry for our cross-country trek. My smile was high-octane, but inside I felt hollow, like an empty plastic bag. Because withholding my truth was such a reflexive response, the emptiness I felt inside was totally normal to me. I didn't take it as a signal that something was off. I simply bypassed the uncomfortable feeling and moved my attention to something else.

Growing up in a community where we weren't allowed to have needs of our own, I came by fawning honestly (we all do with these different survival responses). As a kid on the Ranch, I watched grown-ups around me bend over backward to please the Guru, avoiding her wrath by hiding their true feelings. The blueprint for pleasing was ingrained deep in the recesses of my subconscious mind, ready to save me from the heartbreak of vulnerably expressing my needs in relationships and having them remain unmet.

To be clear, you needn't grow up in a new age commune to develop a killer instinct for fawning. Anyone whose caretakers or childhood environment were unpredictable (read: pretty much *every* middle or high school), emotionally negligent, or volatile, could become a superstar fawner. This survival skill is potent and can be the quickest route to safety and power, especially for people who are traditionally marginalized: girls, women, and LGBTQ+ and BIPOC communities.

In our patriarchal society, where assertive men tend to dominate the higher echelons of power, it can be safer to stay small, pleasing, nice, and helpful. Fawning is especially useful in situations of domestic violence, kidnapping, or sexual assault—anytime we need to persuade someone to like us so we can escape danger. But as humans with a basic need to belong, we revert to fawning in many more instances than the terrifying ones I just mentioned. Fawning is one of the most socially rewarded survival instincts of all time—other people *love* it when we fawn over them. We can amass friendships, money, coveted jobs, romances, and awards . . . and all you have to trade is your truth—if you even know what that is.

Following my enthusiastic response, Liam moved with me to L.A. After a few months of sharing my bedroom, he thankfully found an apartment of his own in Brentwood. One fabulously sunny day, we were driving back home to my place on the Pacific Coast Highway from a friend's wedding in Cambria. I was sitting in the passenger seat of his black Tahoe when my cell phone rang.

"Do you have a blond girlfriend you could bring in and audition with for *Race*?" Chad, a new friend and casting agent for *The Amazing Race*, asked me.

Race was a CBS adventure travel show I'd dreamed of competing in since I first laid eyes on it in high school.

This is it, I thought.

Lately, I'd been waking up at night with thoughts sprinting through my head and a weight on my chest telling me that

I *should* be doing more with my life. I'd quit my highly anticipated PR job at Bragman Nyman Cafarelli (BNC) after only three months. I'd felt trapped by the monotonous hours in the office and longed to be out in the world. Since leaving my "real job," I'd been waiting tables to make rent money at a place near the Santa Monica pier. I needed something big to prove to the world and myself that I wasn't wasting my life. I was *more* than a charismatic waitress.

My insides began doing double backflips. *Be cool, Parv. Don't let on how much you want this.*

"I have two," I said as calmly as I could. The bright blue glittering sea out of my window cheered me on as it whizzed by.

"Great. Bring them both to the hotel in Santa Monica in a week," he said.

Full-body giggles rose from the depths of my belly— champagne bubble happiness. I was *starving* for adventure. Big opportunities like this were the *entire* reason I moved across the country to begin with.

The following week, I showed up as instructed with my two beautiful blond friends. They were both my roommates at the time: Julea, my former waitressing buddy from college, was a go-getter who had charted the most efficient courses around L.A. with her giant, spiral-bound map the first week we'd arrived; and Lily, who was a hilarious, blue-eyed babe with a charming Southern drawl who was always cracking self-deprecating jokes. They were both brilliant, and easy to love.

The afternoon we filed into the glass elevator our nervous

energy filled the space inside, fizzing like pop rocks as we headed to the top floor. I spun around in my strappy flowered sundress to check out my butt in the reflection of the polished gold doors. *Looks okay to me.* This was a big moment. We'd all graduated from the University of Georgia and moved to L.A. to fulfill our dreams. We didn't know what our dreams really were or how we would make them happen, but this *Amazing Race* audition seemed like a nod and a wink from fate. We were on the right track.

The butterflies in my belly intensified, and I buzzed inside, but you wouldn't know by looking at me. On the outside I looked totally cool, completely unfazed by the gravity of this event. My fawn response was automatic; it tightened around my insides like a corset hiding any fear. I was shaking like a leaf, but I would never admit I was scared. Not even to myself. Fear and vulnerability weren't my brand, so no matter how freaked out I was about something, I slapped a smile on my face and dialed up the charm. I was the sunny, happy-go-lucky, Southern cutie. My mask had been moving mountains for me since I started putting it on during my teenage years.

We were directed to the penthouse suite and greeted by a tiny-framed, bubbly bleached-blond casting associate with a cute nose, walkie-talkie in hand and a headset. She looked frazzled if not a little frantic. *Girl, lay off the espresso.* I wanted her to calm down, not so much for her, but for me.

She eyed me up and down as if I were a prized show pony. Then she gave a quick side-eye to Julea and Lily, who stood off to my left. *That's weird.*

"Who are you going in with?" she asked me.

"Chad told me to bring them both," I replied.

"Umm . . . okay." She looked at me like I had green scales and fidgeted nervously with her walkie-talkie. *What am I missing? Why is* she *so nervous? She's already got the job!*

Quickly stuffing down a sharp pang of responsibility I felt for my girlfriends, I gave them an *I-don't-know* shrug. They shrugged back. Nervous Girl flung open one of the double doors and disappeared. The three of us waited like baby birds whose mama flew off with no explanation. The holding pattern we now found ourselves in only served to dial up our collective heat.

Nervous Girl returned. There was movement, we could breathe again.

"All three of you are going in together," she said.

That's right. Now, she's getting it.

"Great!" I beamed, batting my eyes and shining my brightest light at her. Fawn city, baby! I was determined to make her love me. High energy, tap dance, shimmy, smile, wave—whatever you want, I got it. I can do it all!

The three of us stepped into the expansive suite. The entryway was dark. There were stacks of papers, file folders, and a jumble of walkie-talkies messily strewn on the table. We walked deeper inside toward the brightly lit sitting room. The large windows allowed for lots of natural light to spill in and showed an expansive view of Santa Monica. The spaciousness calmed me a bit. I wasn't trapped.

There were three chairs positioned in a row across from the couch. A glass coffee table between the couch and the chairs made the tiniest energetic barrier—*a little more safety*—

between us and the casting director. I thanked God for the table, as if it could prevent the three of us from being exposed as sitting ducks. On the couch sat the casting director, a dark-haired, small-framed goddess who could make or destroy our futures in a single decision. She radiated certainty and an air of authority—another guru with power over me. I felt a familiar smallness in her presence. I wanted so badly to impress her.

"I'm the casting director. Nice to meet you," she said to us.

"Hi, thanks for having us. We're so excited!" we chimed back, our words tumbling over one another. We were still those baby birds, beady-eyed with excitement, now with mouths wide open—each of us hoping Mama Bird would choose our own mouth to feed first. *Charm meter dialed up to 1,000.*

Then her expression turned serious, and she looked directly at me. "Which one do you want to play with?" she asked.

Huh? I was startled. "What? You're the casting director, isn't that your job?" I asked, desperately hoping she would just interview us all and then make the choice.

"You want to win, don't you?"

"Yes." My whole body nodded in agreement.

"Well, which one would you win with?" she asked matter-of-factly. No part of me wanted to cut one of my best friends. But right there in front of them, that's what was being asked of me. *Well, I aim to please.* Without giving it a second thought, I grinned.

"Julea," I said.

The casting director settled back in her seat, satisfied. Lily sunk down in her chair, deflated and betrayed. And internally, I panicked. *What have I done? Lily is going to hate me forever.*

Without another word, the casting director excused us all.

It was a moment of pure survival. Fawn response in full glory. The casting director dangled the keys to the kingdom and all I had to do to claim my castle was drop-kick my baby bird bestie out of the nest and watch her land with a thump. I'd shown the staff I would do what it took to get ahead, a key ingredient they were looking for in a player on the show. I'd gotten in the door of casting, but it was this move that kept me in the room.

I was cutthroat. Like a winner.

We walked out of the casting room and rode the glass elevator down in complete silence. Lily stared straight ahead, her jaw clamped shut. I couldn't bring myself to look at her. My guts twisted up in knots. I felt horrible. I had single-handedly killed her dream. That night I went for a walk to escape the tension in my house. It was cold and windy on the beach, but I didn't notice. Inside I couldn't help but burn with excitement.

A few weeks later, I got a call. I had just clocked in for my waitressing shift at the restaurant when I saw the CBS number on my phone. My hands were shaking as I answered.

"We loved you, Parvati, but the network didn't think you were the right fit for *Race*," the casting associate said, crushing my soul in one sentence. I hung up the phone, devastated. Not only had I done irreparable damage to my friendship with Lily during the casting process but now it felt like my life had no purpose, adventure, or direction. Again. I was back to being a rejected waitress in a sea of wannabe actors in L.A. *I'm a walking cliché.* I fake smiled and flirted my way through my shift, pocketed my wad of tips, and slunk home. Adrift in an ocean of despair.

Three months later, I ended things with Liam for good. I also moved out of the house I shared with Julea and Lily. The awkwardness I had brought into our dynamic never went away, and so it felt like it was my time to leave. I needed to be on my own, so I set up shop in an old, one-bedroom, warehouse-type apartment in West Hollywood. One day not long after I moved in, my phone rang. I was sitting on my bed with Max, a new L.A. girlfriend of mine, gushing about a cute bartender I had a crush on.

I didn't recognize the number, but I picked it up anyway. It was the casting director from the hotel. "Have you ever seen the show *Survivor*?" she asked me.

"Is that the show where people eat bugs?" I replied.

"That's the one," she said.

"Yeah, I don't think I've seen it, but I know it."

"Would you want to do it?" she asked. She told me more about the show. It took place on an island where people were divided into teams and would have to rely on one another to survive while also competing against their fellow tribe mates in challenges. They would vote people out until there were two or three left standing—and finally, a jury of previously eliminated contestants would vote for the winner. It sounded cool to me.

I glanced at Max, who was perched on the edge of my bed beside me. Something major was happening. I mouthed to her, *Do I want to do* Survivor?

"Yes!" She elbowed me with her trademark enthusiasm.

"Okay, yes," I said to the casting director.

"Great," she said, then started spouting off directions. "Make a tape. I'll send you the application to fill out. Then, next week you'll come to the hotel for casting. You'll spend a week there and won't be able to leave for any reason. So, get the time off work and prepare yourself."

"Cool. See you in a week!" I was pumped and a little unsure of what I was getting myself into. But inside, my resolve kicked in. I had been *chosen*. I *belonged* to a group of special ones. A surge of power and confidence welled up inside me. My existence felt validated.

I didn't understand then that my spontaneous and casual *yes* would open the door to an adventure that would take me deep into my own shadow and change my life forever.

3

Fight

"**Y**ou're a rat!" I spat in the direction of Jonathan's face.

It was pitch-black when we returned home from tribal council, after my once-friend had turned on me and voted out my number one ally, Nate. We'd been playing *Survivor*—sleeping in dirt and eating less than nothing for twenty-seven days—and now my best friend was gone because I had trusted the wrong guy. I was pissed.

"I understand you're angry but that's no reason to call me names," Jonathan responded in a tone of moral superiority that made my blood boil.

Being blindsided by a person I'd connected with and looked at as a father figure shocked me and cut me to the core.

I felt out of control in a way I never had before. My rage surprised and overwhelmed me. Until then, I had always been capable of managing myself, believing that showing feelings of anger or being upset was a sign of weakness. But in this moment—starving, dirty, and alone—I was overtaken by the force of my feelings. I couldn't stop the tidal wave of hateful words spewing out of my mouth.

Survivor was shaping up to be an experience full of firsts—first time having to fend for myself on a deserted island; contending with what it felt like to be making a television show with cameras in my face constantly; it was also my first deep experience with betrayal. When I agreed to play, I hadn't given much thought to strategy. I didn't think I would get attached to a group of strangers I'd just met. I was drawn to the adventure and simplicity of living on an island in the South Pacific for thirty-nine days. I'd fantasized about being shipwrecked, and here was my dream coming true. The *Survivor* bubble I found myself in was its own special world, unique and rare. There were no phones, no computers, no signs of civilization at all—it was paradise. I relished sleeping on the bare earth, waking to the sounds of birds and sunshine in my eyes. Wandering down to the ocean for a morning dip, I'd dunk my head under the cool water, hushing the sounds of the world above. I was a mermaid, living free and easy. In the afternoon, I'd sit around camp laughing with my new friends—the only ones who understood this life—while the smell of wood fire and smoke blanketed my body. At night, we'd cuddle up on the hard bamboo raft under the darkest night sky, savoring the beauty of the Milky Way and millions of stars. Other days, I discovered that I enjoyed taking on the role of provider. I'd go out on my own, bringing my wooden bucket to the big lava rocks to hunt for giant snails. I can't say I returned to an enthusiastic response. Nobody loved snails. But something about finding food in nature made me feel self-satisfied and proficient. My heart was wide open, and my confidence was growing alongside my connection to the earth.

My openness also allowed for a vulnerability I didn't anticipate. I didn't know how to keep my heart unguarded and protected at the same time, so I had given full and total trust to my allies—a rookie mistake. When Jonathan betrayed me and voted out Nate, I was enraged simply because I had been so unguarded. My first experience of betrayal was happening on international television, and underneath my rage was a broken heart. I'd been hurt by friends and boyfriends before, but not like this. Never had someone pretended to be my friend by day and then lied to me so brutally by night. No matter that it was a "game," nothing had ever felt so real to me.

Audiences around the world would see me expressing my outrage, but I couldn't think about that. I felt exposed, like I'd been sliced open for all to see the liquid lava that filled my insides. I could only see one way forward: Get rid of the rat.

The anger didn't subside the next day. Without Nate to help talk through my feelings, there was no cooling off for me. I grabbed a coconut and the machete and started chopping angrily. Pieces of coconut went flying in the air around me.

"I'm pretending this is Jonathan's head," I said with a laugh to Becky and Sundra, the women who'd pulled Jonathan into their group to blindside me the night before.

Chop. Thump. Whack.

"Aeeeiiiii!" I screamed. The machete had missed the coconut and struck the tip of my thumb, slicing diagonally
through my thumbnail. When I saw the blood, my knees
buckled. I suddenly felt faint.

The girls rushed to my side. "Call the medic! Parvati's
hurt!" they yelled.

It didn't take long for help to arrive. Sundra held my head
in her lap and Becky sat on the other side of me, speaking in
a soothing tone. I was grateful and touched by the women's
care. Just the night before, they had been my enemies, aligned
with Jonathan to eliminate my friend. It felt like the emotional
and mental terrain was changing rapidly, like whiplash. It
seemed there would be no time for holding grudges in this
game.

"I'm going to stitch up your thumb now," the medic announced.

He put a shot of something in my thumb to numb it and
set to work. I squeezed Becky's hand and took a deep breath.
I'd never had stitches before—another first on the island.

He bandaged my thumb, and now that I couldn't see the
wound, it was easier to tell myself I was fine. *Wait, am I fine?* I
couldn't see anything very well. Just then, I realized I'd forgot-
ten to put my contacts in. My grubby fingers mixed with dirt
and antiseptic gingerly opened the container. I squeezed the
disposable lens between my index finger and bandaged thumb
and shoved it in my eye. Much better.

The game continued, and we hustled off to compete in
the day's challenge. Jeff Probst, the show's host, asked what

happened to my finger. I put my game face back on and told him how I'd injured myself with a smile. Then came another twist. "Your loved ones are here," Jeff said. "Parvati, say hi to your dad, Mike."

Seeing my dad jogging out of the jungle, looking like Jeff Probst's slightly older brother in a blue shirt, melted me. The only food I'd consumed in the past weeks was a few handfuls of coconut and some fish. My clothes were tattered rags hanging off my bony frame. My hips were bruised from sleeping on the hard dirt, and we all reeked of mildew, body odor, and campfire. When I'd been backed against the wall by my enemies, I'd dug my heels in and fought. The competition had brought out a side of me made of earth and grit—I had become a primal cave creature. Dad didn't mind my stench. He hugged me tight, and I felt my shoulders release. Real warmth and affection softened my tight muscles. I hadn't realized how much I was holding in. Dad and I won the reward challenge and enjoyed a feast with a couple lucky castaways and their loved ones that he chose to join us. The ecstatic high of winning and eating immediately following my lowest low of the betrayal and my injury made me feel manic.

But spending time with my dad and having a full stomach brought me back to myself. After he left, I was able to have calm, rational conversations with the people who'd been aligned against me, convincing them it was better to keep me in the game over Jonathan. I shared the leftover food from the reward with them. My generosity plus the injury made me enough of a sympathetic character that they were willing to vote out Jonathan at the next tribal. I was still voted out the following night, but getting Jonathan back felt like a sweet little victory.

After all was said and done, I'd unearthed a broader emotional landscape within myself. In addition to the happy-go-lucky girl I always knew myself to be, I found I could play with other, more intense feelings. Life had brought me lessons of betrayal, raging anger, and a loss of innocence. I'd also recognized my own strength and experienced my primal nature. Maybe I wasn't just a good girl after all. I was changed.

Survivor Cook Islands premiered on September 14, 2006, a week before my twenty-third birthday. My friends threw a party for me at a bar called The Terrace on Washington Ave. in Marina Del Rey. Walking into the packed room, electricity coursed through my body. It was crowded with people who were all very excited to see me on TV. My high school dream was coming true. As a kid who barely watched TV on the commune, I could have never imagined this. I could not stop smiling.

I'd brought Alex with me to the party; he was a bartender at one of the nightclubs in Hollywood I worked at. We'd been flirting before I left for *Survivor* but started officially dating when I got home from the show. My best friend, Max, had picked me up from the airport the night my plane landed from Cook Islands, and we'd immediately met up with Alex and his friends at a party in the Hills.

"I have something for you." Alex's brown eyes twinkled as he handed me a bouquet of dead roses. "I got one for every day you were gone. Isn't that romantic?"

I nodded. "Weird. But yeah, romantic I guess."

Alex was an actor—or really, he was a bartender who occasionally auditioned for acting gigs. He stunned like a Disney prince with lean muscles, dark hair, and brooding dark eyes. He'd recently played a leading role in an indie rom-com I'd never heard of, and he just knew he was going to be a Major Star. When *Survivor* began airing, I started getting loads of attention. At brunch with Alex, people would walk up to our table and ask for a picture and an autograph—mine, not his. Though he never admitted it, Alex was jealous of the attention I was getting.

"I guess it's fine for *you* to do reality TV," he would say to me condescendingly. "I'm a *real actor*. I would never do that. Reality TV would ruin my reputation."

I tolerated his rude comments because I was getting used to people being mean to me. Sometimes people who recognized me from the show would say how much they loved me, but a lot of other times they would tell me things like: "We love to hate you at our house" or "We were so happy when you got voted out, you were the most annoying one out there."

Comments like these rocked me. I had no indication on the island that anyone disliked me. Although I'd been an outsider in the end, the people I played with treated me with kindness in the game. I'd gone from living through one of the most embodied and powerfully transformative experiences of my life to becoming a one-dimensional character in a box, on display for all to judge. It was fun getting recognized, but I never knew what to expect so I hardened my insides, unwilling to give their words a soft place to land.

On top of Alex's nasty remarks, journalists who reviewed the show called me "slutty" and characterized me as a "vapid whore." Though I hadn't hooked up with anyone on the island, I had used the flirty-fawning strategy I'd practiced in high school to create relationships and advance my game. But in my mind this was game play. The intensity of the backlash confused me. I'd always seen myself as a likable person. I'd been accepted and invited into diverse social groups with ease. I couldn't make sense of the harsh criticism I was receiving from simply being myself and playing a game. *But, if so many people are saying those mean things, including the boy who loves me, then they must be true*, I thought. I started to believe the mean comments, and I began to lose my inherent sense of being likable. I felt ugly inside.

Maybe in a way, I wanted Alex to be mean, so I could have someone to fight with. He was a real live flesh-and-blood opponent I could see, unlike the faceless critics taking shots at me from behind their computer screens. Since wrapping Cook Islands, my body had remained in defensive mode. The fight I'd had on the island with Jonathan had never been resolved, even though I'd "gotten even" with him by voting him out of the game. The fight chemistry—adrenaline and stress hormones—was still alive and stewing inside me. I was a bubbling cauldron of heat and repressed anger, though outwardly I performed "happy." It makes sense that after I came home, I ran right into the arms of a mean boyfriend who could argue back.

Each time someone said something nasty to me, I felt heat rise up within me. But instead of feeling righteous and expressing my anger like I'd done in Cook Islands when I was upset about my friend Nate's elimination, I felt embarrassed. I was ashamed that I'd let Jonathan get to me. I felt silly and weak over losing control of myself in the game, and I didn't want to let that happen again. I didn't want anyone to have the power to hurt me. So I pushed down the anger, locking it away in a deep dark dungeon where it would never see the light of day. I was impenetrable, an unbreakable fortress of strength like Buffy the Vampire Slayer.

I was taught to handle anger this way. In my childhood at the Ranch, only the Guru was allowed to feel or express anger or aggression. Her anger was a sign of strength, a show of her power over others. It had a purpose, she was "protecting people" with her rage. Everyone else had to suppress it, take the hit, go with the flow, and paint an agreeable smile on their face—for us, not reacting was a show of strength.

My upbringing led me to believe anger and rage needed to be exiled. The only time Ranch dwellers were permitted to show aggression was during the tae kwon do tournaments they often competed in. This was the sole appropriate arena to fight, dominate, and overpower another person. Both my parents were black belts. In the dojo, they could unleash, and they did, winning trophies for the glory of the Ranch. When my family moved to Georgia, we kept the tradition going. My parents enrolled my sister and me into tae kwon do, and I loved it—sparring with bigger boys and breaking wooden boards with my fists was fun.

I'd grown up with all of this, and I followed the rules like a good girl, keeping my aggressive, messy feelings contained to the appropriate time and place. I ditched tae kwon do after middle school, but in college I'd taken up boxing. I found a gym on the outskirts of town and met a trainer named Raymond, a former heavyweight champ. I loved learning how to throw my body weight into a punch to make it land hard. I'd leave the gym drenched in sweat, fully relieved of any angst or anxiety I'd felt before—I was a relaxed noodle.

After moving to L.A., I still craved the release and power I got from boxing. When I was working as a waitress in Santa Monica, I met a girl who told me about a gym that belonged to the famous folk singer Bob Dylan. It was a hidden treasure tucked away underneath a synagogue. Kinda like one of those speakeasies, you could only find it if you had the inside scoop. The moment you walked in, you knew you were somewhere special—a boxing gym, but make it glam. The floor was covered in leopard-print carpet. There were two plush stilettos for chairs and a ring in the center, heavy bags hung by its side and a couple speed bags on the wall. I started training there a few months before I left to play *Survivor*.

When I got home after the show, I went into recovery mode, eating and numbing my feelings—gorging on ice cream, pizza, and quesadillas and lounging on the couch bingeing *Gossip Girl*. After about a month of this, I was itching to get back into the boxing gym. My body was tightly wound and my fuse was short. I'd been sidestepping my anger, distracting myself with food, alcohol, and aggressive sex, but those coping strategies were only making me feel worse about myself. I felt out of control and a little lost. The boxing gym was a safe place for me to release the aggression I was holding and rebuild my confidence.

"She's back!" My trainer, Brian, beamed at me as I walked in.

"Did you miss me?" I said flirtatiously and threw my arms around him. Brian was my coach. We connected instantly from the moment I first walked into the gym about a year prior. He was tall, with close-cropped light brown hair, blue eyes, and a handsome face. Best of all, he had a genuine enthusiasm for training me. He said I showed real potential and encouraged me to fight in matches. The idea of fighting other people *for real* sent a thrill up my spine. But Brian made me feel like I could do it.

There were other women in the gym who fought in matches, and I trained with them, doing drills with the speed bags and heavy bags. We put our headgear on and mouthpieces in and entered the ring. I was channeling my aggression into something strong and helpful. It wasn't bad or shameful to be aggro in this arena, it was productive. I refined my technique, bobbing and weaving, throwing jabs and hard right crosses. I didn't hold back—landing body shots, knocking the wind out of my sparring partners and dropping them to the floor. They didn't take it easy on me either. They'd hit me in the head with full intensity, spinning my body sideways. A *whoosh* of anger would rise, and I'd exhale hard a few times to settle myself down. It wasn't personal here. It was business. Unlike *Survivor*, where betrayal blurred the rules of friendship, the rules of the ring were clear to me, aggression and technique were rewarded. At the end of a sparring match, when the bell rang, we'd touch gloves and hug. No hard feelings.

By giving me a safe space to feel and release my anger, without me knowing it, boxing was healing me.

I was hooked—and eagerly wanted to participate in my first match. Day after day, I entered the gym with that goal in mind, training with full focus for months.

The crowd in the stands of the Hollywood nightclub cheered wildly. My fight song, "Hollaback Girl" by Gwen Stefani, bumped from the speakers and bright lights flashed in my eyes as I pushed my body between the parted ropes and entered the boxing ring. My heart raced and my legs tingled as I shed my silky blue robe and sized up my competition. My opponent, Kimberly the Crusher, stood in the opposite corner. Kimberly was a whopping five foot ten inches—much taller than my five-five frame—and weighed in at ten pounds heavier than me. *Okay, so she's bigger than me, but she looks scared.* I'd been training in the gym three days a week, conditioning, hitting the heavy bag, working the mitts with my trainer, and sparring with the other girls on my team. I felt *un-crushable.*

Ding ding ding!

The starting bell rang, and I darted out toward The Crusher, fueled by adrenaline, enthusiasm, and the will to win. I threw mad punches. Jab. Jab. Right cross. Left hook. Uppercut. Uppercut. The crowd went wild. The Crusher retreated to her corner and spun around to get away from me. You *never* turn your back on your opponent in the ring. I had her on the ropes. After two more rounds, the fight was over. I had won.

Boxing took the edge off my short fuse and gave me my power back. It gave me a safe way to express aggression, and I was rewarded when I won with a bag full of cash. In every other arena of life, I cared desperately about being liked, looking good, and being attractive to the opposite sex, but in the ring, I could be mean. I could be ugly. I could hit back. It was okay if my opponent didn't like me, my job was to beat them up. In a way, I bundled up the anger I felt toward Jonathan, the mean journalists, Alex, and myself and took it all out on my opponent in the ring. Matches were medicine. As long as a fight was contained in an arena where everyone understood and agreed to the rules, I could throw myself into it with every ounce of my fearsome warrior power.

A year later, when *Survivor* called me to go back for a second time, I was ready to win. My boxing training had refined my ability to self-soothe and contain my anger and aggression. This time around, I'd anticipate betrayal and I'd beat people to the punch. I'd also get Lasik eye surgery so I wouldn't have to deal with dirty contact lenses or blurry puzzles. My additional game prep included reading books like *The 48 Laws of Power* and *The Art of Persuasion*. I gave myself full permission to do the nasty things I'd have to do to win the game: lie, manipulate, backstab, and be selfish. Things I'd never permit myself to do consciously in my day-to-day regular life. I was a good girl, but I knew I'd have to be bad to win, and I was okay with it. Besides, my body was already living inside a potent cocktail of survival chemistry, the adrenaline and cortisol that came alongside flight, fawn, and fight. I was poised for victory. *Survivor* would simply be a continuation of what I was already doing in my daily life.

When I hit the beach this time, I knew what to expect physically. I remembered the sore hips from sleeping on hard dirt; the rats that danced around underneath our feet at night; the funky, musty smell of damp clothes and firewood smoke; the chill that seeped into my bones and wouldn't leave.

Though physically prepared, I underestimated the emotional toll playing with my new level of intensity would take. It was harder this time around. I didn't have the same innocent naivety that had buoyed me the first time.

By day I schemed with my trusted confidante, a gorgeous, doe-eyed, twentysomething brunette named Amanda. At night my mind couldn't let go; I dreamed that bullets were raining down and I dodged them by hiding behind cars and barrels. My hypervigilance became my bodyguard, always watching, always thinking three steps ahead.

When I was tribe-swapped away from Amanda and my other closest ally, Cirie, I was afraid. The deck had been reshuffled, and it didn't look good for me. Eliza had wanted me out since day one, and she was in my new tribe along with Jonathan, the man who'd betrayed me in my previous *Survivor* experience. But I saw an opportunity to pull two new girls, Natalie and Alexis, into our alliance.

"Eliza is trying to get rid of Alexis," I lied to them on a walk in the jungle. Alexis looked at me, terrified. My stomach jolted with a little hit of electricity. I liked playing with good, clean emotional manipulation; making up a bold-faced lie complicated things and was wildly uncomfortable. But this one felt necessary. I needed these girls on my side, and I knew Natalie was a protector who would go to the ends of the earth to keep Alexis safe.

"What!" Natalie was pissed. "She's dead," she said with conviction.

I have them.

"Agreed. Let's get rid of Eliza. I've got Cirie and Amanda. They'll work with us when we merge, and we can carve a path to the end," I said.

I kept my promise and brought together a formidable all-female alliance. Together, as the Black Widow Brigade, we blindsided Eliza first and then systematically eliminated the men one by one. Working this way with a strong group of women felt magical and fun. We cackled and stirred the imaginary pot, relishing in our witchy powers. Every day I woke up grateful that I had a group of smart, savvy allies I could trust like this. But a wrench was thrown into our plans when Erik Reichenbach, an ice-cream scooper from Hell, Michigan, won individual immunity in the final five. His victory meant either Natalie, Cirie, Amanda, or I would be voted out, and my dream of an all-female final four would be lost. We were in mourning, until Cirie threw out a wild thought.

"Do you think we could get Erik to give the immunity necklace to Natalie?" she asked, half joking.

I felt the wind shift and lifted my head. We absolutely could do that.

Each member of the BWB would play a key role in Operation Immunity Necklace: Natalie was the damsel in distress, looking for a hero; Cirie was the mama bear, a place for Erik to come for wise counsel; Amanda was the good cop, helping Erik to see that he needed to redeem himself in the eyes of the jury by making a big, bold play; and I was bad cop, the one who told Erik how he'd messed up and that there was no way out for him. And I would be the target for everyone to throw votes on. All day, each one of us played our parts like Academy Award–winning actors. By the time we got to tribal council that night, Erik was hypnotized. Around the fire, the performance continued throughout Jeff's pre-vote questioning.

"I want to give individual immunity to Natalie," Erik said as he placed the necklace over her head. I glanced over at the jury. Eyes bulged, mouths hung open in disbelief. James put his head in his hands. I sat behind Erik and smiled.

With that, we voted Erik out—making *Survivor* history with our all-female final four.

Back at camp, we celebrated, but the game wasn't over. I still had to make it to the final two and plead my case to the jury. I fought hard, physically willing myself to go on. Though

I never let it show, playing the bad guy with Erik and blindsiding Ozzy and James took a toll on me emotionally and mentally. I felt a bit of guilt for crushing their hearts. On top of that, I was laser-focused on maintaining my social bonds and keeping myself in the number one spot with each person in my alliance so, no matter what, I was making it to the end. I stood on the front lines, taking hits for the team, never going on any rewards and eating very little the entire game. Who needed food anyway? I was a professional sufferer. It was in my genes. I would earn my victory through sheer grit and strategy.

In the end, my social prowess and friendship with Amanda earned me a spot in the final two. I sat on my stump, ragged, weary, filthy, and proud of myself—stoically absorbing jabs from bitter jury members who wanted to hurt me like I had hurt them.

"How does it feel to choose greed over friendship? I want you to do an interpretive dance to demonstrate how it feels to choose greed," Ozzy asked, attempting to shame and humiliate me. I contracted a bit on my stump. *Did I do that? Isn't this a game that everyone is trying to win?*

"I think you're just a mean girl," Eliza said. I stared blankly back, still armored from playing the game. Nothing would seep in. I was in survival mode.

After the final tribal council was over, we went to Ponderosa, the camp where the jury had been staying since leaving the game. When I weighed in, I'd lost fifteen pounds. I showered and washed thirty-nine days of dirt out of my hair, watching the warm water turn brown around my feet.

The scented soap softened something in me, and I felt less animal, more human. Alone for the first time in weeks, I let go of the emotion that had been building inside. Big fat tears streamed down my face, and I let them, relieved I had a safe space to cry. I didn't have to hide what I was feeling anymore.

The winner wouldn't be announced immediately. We'd have to wait another six months for the live finale when the votes were counted.

When I got home from competing on *Survivor: Micronesia*, I was surprised to find that I couldn't fight anymore. My first day back at the boxing gym I suited up, ready to spar. The bell rang and I stepped toward my opponent. But I felt suffocated inside my headgear. *Why can't I breathe?* She landed an easy punch to my head. My vision blurred and I dropped to the floor. I stood up, ripped my headgear off, and ran out of the gym, dazed and dizzy. I had a panic attack in the parking lot. After that, I decided not to go back to boxing.

I didn't know it at the time but looking back on this moment with the knowledge I have now of the nervous system, I can see that my body's capacity to field an attack was completely shot. My stress tolerance was so reduced from the intensity of playing *Survivor* at the level I played for thirty-nine days that I had no ability to cope with threat—either real or perceived. If someone came toward me aggressively, even in a controlled environment like the gym, my body's response was to shut down, or instinctively run away, not stand and fight. To heal this and regain my strength, I needed safety.

But I didn't have safe spaces or secure relationships built into my life at the time, and when *Survivor: Micronesia* aired, I faced even more criticism from the public. One journalist from *Entertainment Weekly* wrote in his column: "I can't believe it was the locals showing Parvati how to catch crabs and not the other way around." The remarks that cut the deepest were when people called me a slut and said I was a bad example for young girls. I had made it to the final two on *Survivor* by bringing powerful, attractive, intelligent women together and creating a women's alliance that systematically voted out fan-favorite men. We led some notorious blindsides, including the epic one with Erik the ice-cream scooper. I had been unapologetic about using flirtation on both the men and women in my tribe as a primary tactic to get what I wanted. People were angry with me for this, and frankly I think they were scared something like that could happen to them in their own lives if they trusted a woman.

Clearly, I was a polarizing character and people had no problem coming up to me in the street and telling me how they felt about me.

"Are you Parvati?" asked the woman next to me in Santa Monica dispensing frozen yogurt into her bowl.

"Yes." I smiled at her.

"My husband and I can't stand the sound of your voice," she said, and smirked as she walked away. My vision blurred. I just absorbed the gut punch and sat down with my friends, pretending like nothing happened. Comments like these left me stunned and confused. *Why am I so reviled?*

The live finale for *Survivor: Micronesia* took place in a packed theater in New York City. All the former contestants traveled there, and it was the first time many of us had seen one another since filming on the island.

Onstage they'd made a replica of the final tribal council with the jury sitting to our left around a fake fire pit, Amanda and I front and center facing Jeff's podium. The theater was filled with friends, relatives, and fans. My parents, my sister, and my little brother sat in the second row cheering me on.

The audience jumped to their feet, screaming and clapping as Jeff walked down the aisle holding the votes. Taking his place onstage he said, "Amanda, Parvati, Jury. I gotta say, the fans are saying this is perhaps the best season of *Survivor* we've ever had. So, kudos to you guys." Amanda and I looked at each other, proud of our efforts, but anxious to find out which of us would be taking home the title of Sole Survivor.

"All right, the contestants have waited a long time to find out the winner of *Survivor: Micronesia: Fans vs. Favorites,* and now it's time. There are eight votes in here, you only need five to win. I'll read the votes," Jeff announced.

I held my breath and clutched both of Amanda's hands.

One vote Parvati. One vote Amanda. He pulled out another vote: Parvati. Another one: Amanda. Parvati. Amanda.

"We're tied three to three," Jeff stated to the audience. My legs were shaking. I could barely contain my nerves.

The energy in the theater was electric. Two votes left—

one more for Parvati. "If the next vote is Amanda, we have a tie. If it's for Parvati, we have a winner," Jeff explained. He unfolded the last vote. "The winner of *Survivor: Fans vs. Favorites:* Parvati." Jeff smiled at me. "Go hug your family."

My mouth fell open. Amanda and I pulled each other in for a huge embrace. I looked at her, shocked. "You just won a million dollars!" she squealed. I could barely believe it. Gratitude filled my heart, and I hugged the jury members who'd voted for me, then I floated down the stairs to squeeze my mom, dad, sister, and brother. All of my hard work had paid off. I'd won. On *CBS This Morning,* they handed me a check for a million dollars, which I promptly shoved in my bag. I was on cloud nine after my big victory and a full day of press, radio interviews, and a *People* magazine shoot. I trotted around JFK airport like a show pony, beaming at anyone who looked my way. *It's a long flight back to L.A.,* I thought. *I should get food.* I grabbed a sandwich from a little shop.

"Your card is declined. Do you have another form of payment?" the cashier asked.

"Oh, yeah," I said, a little embarrassed, and handed them my debit card.

"This one doesn't work either," she said.

"Oh, ummm, never mind then," I said as I sheepishly put the sandwich back on its shelf. Fishing around in my bag, I found eighty-five cents—enough for an orange.

I had a million-dollar check in my bag and couldn't buy a sandwich. *Ironic,* I thought.

SLUT. Entertainment blogger Perez Hilton had his laptop open. He'd scrawled the word in big capital letters over an image of a female celebrity.

Oh, come on. I'm trying to get a coffee.

When I won *Survivor* in 2008, there was no cancel culture. Each morning I walked into the Coffee Bean and Tea Leaf on Sunset Blvd. and saw Perez sitting at his usual table, firing off photos of Britney Spears, Lindsay Lohan, and Mischa Barton all with white letters smeared across their images reading *SLUT. WHORE. PIG.* Witnessing these kinds of character attacks was starting to feel familiar to me. Hilton inspired legions of internet trolls with his crude, misogynistic tactics, including but not limited to bullying and harassing young women, outing people, leaking nude photos, and trashing celebrities' kids. At his peak, his blog was getting upward of eight million readers per day. If anyone was brave enough to speak out against him, he'd ruthlessly decimate them. So, many celebs like Lady Gaga and Paris Hilton took a different approach: fawn. They befriended the jerk so he wouldn't feature them on his blog.

In a similar fashion, there were cruel photos of me circulating. Someone had imitated Perez Hilton's style, taking an image of me from *Survivor* and drawing semen dripping down my face with the word *SLUT* written over my chin. It was horrifying, but totally normal. No one said it was wrong. No one stood up for me or for any of the women Perez was insulting. Instead, people laughed. We were all big, slutty jokes. Now when I think about it, I can see slut-shaming for what it is: a

tool of oppression with the objective of shaming and silencing women. But back then I didn't have this perspective. Instead, I internalized the shame. The message I received: *It's
dangerous to be powerful, successful, and sexy—if you're a woman.* I
didn't understand how women were supposed to embody
strength if a strong woman was so threatening. Though I had
just won one of the hardest game shows in the world, I didn't
feel like a winner. I felt like my core was rotten. I wanted to
run and hide—make myself invisible—just disappear.

Instead of wondering if these loud, mean outside voices
were only projecting their own fear and unprocessed pain on
me, I thought they must be right: I really had done something
terrible, and I deserved to be punished. *Maybe I can redeem myself by being extra nice?* I had always made my way in life by
being pleasing and attractive—my power came from people
liking me. But now that my attractiveness was under threat
from millions of invisible critics, and I was wildly disliked—
where would my value and worth come from?

I needed to do damage control around my public percep-
tion. Getting people to see me as a "good girl" and to approve
of me again became my driving force. So, any anger I felt
about the way I was being treated, I turned inward. I went
back to the old mentality that was instilled in me in the commune, making anger an impermissible feeling. Claiming and
expressing my anger would destroy everything I had built in
my life. And so, I locked it up in some deep dungeon in the pit
of my belly, and then I vacated that part of my body. If I
didn't feel it, I thought, that would surely keep me safe.

I didn't understand the danger of exiling and repressing my rage. Anger, after all, is the emotion that shows us when an injustice has occurred. When I denied my anger, I also severed my connection to my boundaries. Without boundaries and an ability to speak up for or defend myself, I allowed people to troll all over me, depleting my precious reserves even further.

I became trapped inside a vicious internal spiral of self-loathing. My self-hatred had a powerful effect on my choices. Instead of seeking out safe relationships that would have brought me back to a healthier state, I created emotionally destabilizing ones with aggressive, controlling men that provided me with the opportunity to play exciting power games.

One night, out at the nightclub Tao, I was sitting with my latest boyfriend, a film director I'd met before I stopped going to the boxing gym. Our relationship had started off with some feisty sparring in the ring. I liked that he never took it easy on me. We were having sushi and I guess I was giving off a vibe.

"The word I would use to describe you is 'defiant,'" he said.

"I am not!" I argued.

"Why do you always have to be so defiant?" He smirked.

I had gotten so caught in the loop of performing "badass" that I couldn't drop my guard, especially not on a date. Other people saw me as a strong woman, a fighter, but the truth was I was fighting myself. Before *Survivor*, I'd thought I was a good girl, a good friend. I knew myself as a kind person with a caring heart, but I couldn't untangle the game from real life. Ozzy's and the critics' words stuck with me; I felt guilty about blindsiding my friends and helpless to prove I wasn't the awful, greedy, slutty person many people believed me to be. All my feelings melded into a thick, heavy stew. I was confused, lost, and dead scared of people knowing the truth of how I felt about myself.

4

Freeze

"Parvati, you played this game under Russell's thumb, like a spouse in a bad abusive relationship. And you never got out of it. I wanted you to get out. I wanted it so bad for you, and you didn't. I like you, but I can't support that." My castmate Candice's words smacked me in the face.

I opened my mouth to speak, to tell her how wrong she was, how hypocritical she was. Just days ago, *she* had tried to align with Russell and wanted to work with him, but he'd betrayed her. Her speech to me felt unfair and out of line. Tears filled my eyes, but Candice had already turned her back on me and returned to her seat on the jury bench.

Survivor season twenty, *Heroes vs. Villains,* aired in 2010—two years after my winning *Survivor* season. I was twenty-eight and it was my third time playing the game—and it skewered me unlike any other season of *Survivor* I'd ever experienced. This latest season was an all-star cast of twenty people: ten "villains" and ten "heroes" from previous seasons. In a last-minute switch, I was cast in the villains tribe. I believed putting me with the villains had something to do with Amanda, Cirie, and James all being on the heroes tribe and needing to split us up to prevent an unfair advantage.

But I didn't have time to puzzle over it much because on day one I was targeted as the biggest threat. I spent the rest of my thirty-nine days on the island starving and scrapping my way through the game with my trademark endurance and impenetrability. I aligned with the only people who'd work with me: the most notorious *Survivor* villain of all time, Russell Hantz, and a hot, busty brunette named Danielle. Part of me knew I was making a deal with the devil by working with Russell. He could be a controlling bully, but he was also strategic and cunning. He had an amazing ability to read people and knew how to play on emotions, mainly fear. I watched him lie through his teeth like a snake oil salesman and people would buy it. He had Coach, JT, Jerri, and Rupert all wrapped around his stumpy little finger. Russell loved me for some miraculous reason. He was willing to put his game on the line for me like some kind of *Survivor* cowboy. I was grateful for his blind allegiance. When he and I were on the chopping block early in the game, Russell played his immunity idol for me, risking his own elimination. Where others bowed in fear or protested against him, I found I could easily negotiate my relationship with him by throwing him little nuggets of validation here and there. I called him my hero and gave him sweet hugs. The cheap sugar seemed a small price to pay to make it to the end of the game.

My strategy worked, but it wasn't easy. *Heroes vs. Villains* was my first time playing as an underdog. I'd always had a majority position and felt like I'd belonged, but this game was different. I was an outcast working with an outlaw. At the merge, our villains tribe of five united with the heroes tribe of five. I was excited to reconnect with my friends Amanda and Candice, from my previous seasons. I needed some more numbers and thought maybe I could get in with them. But when I tried to talk with them, they ran off in different directions. In fact, everyone did. Turned out, they thought I was running an all-girls alliance again, and people were afraid of being played like the boys in Micronesia—even my former friends Amanda and Candice avoided me for fear of being swept up in the girl-power paranoia. They were in awe of Russell, however. Somehow, he had managed to survive against all odds. He was the belle of the ball, and they all wanted a turn talking with him. Though I knew Russell was working for me, I found myself alone on the sand with a broken heart.

"Parvati, are you okay?" Danielle asked when she saw me sitting down alone.

"Fine," I replied with tears in my eyes.

I was not fine. I felt sad and mad. Fueled by the fury of being shunned, I wanted revenge on all the heroes who'd ignored me, so I set my sights on eliminating them one by one. Before the first tribal council and post-merge, I set up my move. I let my ally Danielle win immunity on a challenge I could have easily won, securing her safety. I had an immunity idol in my bag I'd found on the villains' beach that Russell didn't know about. When we got back from the challenge

Russell gave me his idol, thinking the heroes were targeting me. So I now had two. Then I spoke with Amanda and told her I had an idol, hoping maybe she'd come around and play with me. When she insisted I play it for myself, I told her I would, but I also sensed I couldn't trust her. So, later that night, when I got to tribal council, I sat on my stump knowing the heroes (thinking I'd play my idol for myself) wouldn't vote for me; I was safe. My ally Danielle was safe with the immunity necklace. Russell had ingratiated himself with the heroes; he was safe. That only left two people vulnerable from my five-person villains tribe: Sandra and Jerri. Sandra was funny and I enjoyed hanging with her on the beach, but she despised Russell so I didn't talk strategy with her. Jerri outwardly disliked me. I didn't have solid relationships with either of them, but I wanted to secure the majority, and I knew a grand gesture would score me some serious relational credit. *Was I willing to let go of both of my idols?* The move would leave me completely exposed, and Russell would know I played him. It was risky. *Maybe too risky.*

When the time came, after the votes were cast and before they were read, Jeff asked: "If anyone has an immunity idol and would like to play it, now is the time to do so."

"You know what, Jeff," I piped up, my voice shaking as I pulled the first idol out of my bag, "I think it would be downright depressing to watch green bananas turn yellow without my debaucherous little villains around, so, Sandra, that one's for you." People froze on their stumps. The silence around me felt thick. *Fuck it, I'm going for it.* "And, Jeff"—I pulled the other idol out of my bag—"I'd just like to increase our odds. So,

Jerri, that one's for you too!" I finished with a flourish. Both women got up and played their idols. "These are hidden immunity idols so any votes cast for Sandra or Jerri will not count," Jeff said.

The heroes had voted for Jerri. All their votes didn't count. Us villains had banded together and voted for JT, the leader of the heroes. His exit interview said a lot about the temperature of the game: "This was probably one of the biggest moves in *Survivor* history and it did not go my way. I know that people are villains for a reason; don't ever trust 'em. Worse than that, don't ever trust women, ever, ever, ever. And I knew that. That's why I was so devoted to gettin' rid of those women. And they got me." With my play that night, we gained the majority.

But now I had no idols protecting me; I was perceived as an even bigger threat and Russell was mad at me for keeping my own secret idol. I had a grueling uphill battle to the end.

By day thirty-nine, I found myself sitting in the final three with Russell and Sandra. Sandra had played an under-the-radar game but was very vocal about how much she hated Russell and that she was playing *Survivor* for her family and her husband, who was fighting in Afghanistan. That night the power shifted to the jury—people I'd played with and voted out. They glared at me and Russell, practically salivating for their revenge.

One by one, they rose to speak. Amanda, who'd been my number one ally two years before in *Survivor: Micronesia*, barely acknowledged my existence. When I opened my mouth to defend myself, she held her arm up to silence me. "No. I don't want to hear a word out of you," she said. She *hated* me.

Two other *Survivor* favorites, JT and Rupert, gave searing speeches about how Russell was the worst person of all time. And then there was Candice, my former ally and BFF from my very first experience on *Survivor* in the Cook Islands, saying I had behaved like a victim of domestic abuse by aligning and working with Russell. Their words hit me like an assault, and I sat still on my stump, helpless to stop it—TV cameras trained on me like sniper rifles. All I could do was sit there, shut up, and take it. As each jury member spoke, I felt myself shrink until I was so small I was sure I'd disappeared. I was frozen—unable to think, move, or act. Incapable of doing anything at all.

In today's era of *Survivor*, producers ask about what's happening in contestants' lives outside of the game. They make reels that show some of the things the players are contending with beyond the game that inform their character and help the audience understand them better. If *Heroes vs. Villains* aired today, you might see some of the intensity I'd been dealing with in my life just before I left to play the game. The phone call that would change everything for me is still seared into memory.

"Is this Parvati?" the man's voice on the other end of the phone asked. It was a gorgeous sunny day in L.A. and I had the top down on my convertible sports car. The wind was whipping my hair around my face.

"Yes?" I replied, curious.

"Your brother has been in a skateboarding accident. I found him facedown in a pool of blood. It's lucky I did, too. He would have died. How quickly can you get here?" The voice echoed in my ears.

"This isn't funny," I said. "Put Kaelan on the phone. I don't think this is a funny joke."

"I'm not joking." The man spoke gravely.

I felt my heart catch in my throat.

My fifteen-year-old, shaggy-haired, blue-eyed, skater boy brother Kaelan was on summer vacation and had flown in to stay with me and my sister in our two-bedroom Brentwood apartment for a few days while my parents celebrated our grandfather's birthday in Northern California. I'd left for college when Kaelan was five years old and the only real time we'd spent together was when I'd go home to Georgia for the holidays. Although we weren't together very often, we shared a similar twinkly, mischievous sense of humor and had a unique bond. He was a live wire, bubbling with energy, but he also had a thoughtful way of taking in the world that made him seem shy and endeared him to other people. I was excited to host him and show him how much bigger and brighter life could get for him.

Before he arrived, my mom had called to tell me that there'd been an incident at home—they'd gone out for the night and when they returned, they found Kaelan on the living room floor. He had gotten into their liquor cabinet and drunk himself into a stupor, alone. When they took him to the emergency room, the doctor had laughed it off, saying something like "teenage boys will do this kind of thing." Mom's story went in one ear and out the other. I sided with the doctor, assuring her Kaelan would be fine with us.

My mind refused to make the connection that just a few months prior, my best friend Max's younger brother Luke had died in an alcohol-related boating accident. Her family had a search-and-rescue team dragging the lake for three days before they found him. I'd flown to Texas for emotional support. When divers pulled his body out of the water, I was there. I watched Max's mom crumple in the street like all the bones in her body had turned to dust. When they laid Luke out on the table at the mortuary, I couldn't go inside with Max. She begged me to come in, but my body froze. I hid behind the door, not able to force myself to confront the truth of the tragedy. It was too much for me to bear. I never said anything to Max about the shame and guilt I felt at not being able to move my legs to be with her in that room. I was there to support her, not burden her with my feelings. Max moved back to Texas a month later, and I lost my best friend in L.A., my safety net and my partner in crime.

I was a mess of unprocessed grief after coming home from Texas, and the only way I knew how to cope with my emotional pain was to pack it away, pretend everything was fine, smoke a lot of cigarettes, and drink buckets of vodka. I was in complete denial, and as long as I had something exciting to focus on, I could keep going. I didn't really have time to work anything out anyway, since I'd agreed to go back and play *Survivor*. It had been a year since I'd won *Survivor: Micronesia,* and I was aching for the island. Even though each reentry to the game felt like it sent my nervous system into overdrive, I loved the escape it brought me and how it tested my limits. I couldn't wait to lose myself in a world of competition where the rules were clear. Where I had one point of focus, and I could excel. I needed *Survivor* like a heroin addict needs a fix.

When I picked up Kaelan from LAX, I immediately took him to meet my boyfriend of the moment for a swanky dinner at Geisha House. After that, we snuck him into the Roosevelt for a margarita. The thought of how risky it was to give a person with a potential alcohol problem a drink didn't cross my mind. I was the cool big sister, and I wanted my little brother to have the Hollywood experience. It was getting late when his big blue eyes locked in on mine.

"Can I have another one?" he asked me.

"Nah," I said, suddenly feeling like a responsible, protective older sister. "It's late. We're going home now."

The next morning, I woke up to frantic emails from *Survivor* casting about my wardrobe. I was now a week late getting it to them, and they were threatening to cut me from the game. I threw on some leggings and an oversized T-shirt and told my sister to look after Kaelan, who was still sleeping soundly on the couch.

When I got the call about my brother's accident, I was on my way home with shopping bags of gray and blue clothes and bathing suits for my *Survivor* wardrobe. When the reality of the news hit me, I went into crisis rescue mode. I hit the gas, called my sister and my parents and gave them the update as I drove. Five minutes later, I slammed my black Audi TT into park at a red curb behind the fire truck that had already arrived on the scene; I raced to find my brother at the bottom of a hill in the alley behind my house. He was standing up, leaning on a car.

"Hi, Parv," he said with a half smile. He looked dazed but he knew who I was. I took it as a good sign.

I don't remember if I rode in the ambulance with him to the hospital or how I got there; I only remember sitting in the hospital room with my brother on a bed hooked up to beeping machines and wires in his chest and head. My parents had flown down from San Francisco and my sister was there, too. They were all ash gray.

We were shook.

Later, I left everyone at the hospital in Westwood and drove to the *Survivor* casting office in Brentwood, which was now closed. I took out a black Sharpie, scribbled my name on one of the shopping bags, shoved all my wardrobe inside, and tossed it over the locked gate. On the drive home, my mind was full of tension and fear. *Is my brother going to die?* My fear crowded out any worries about how I'd perform when it was time to compete on *Survivor*. I was on autopilot; checking responsibilities off my list in the midst of chaos gave me a tiny sense of control. I could get through this, one task at a time.

When nighttime finally came and the sky was dark, I slumped on the floor of my balcony with a glass of vodka on ice and a cigarette.

My family and I spent the rest of the week taking shifts at the hospital by my brother's side. When Kaelan was awake, he cracked jokes and made fun of us, his usual trademark mischievous humor still intact, but we got worried when the swelling inside his skull wasn't going down. The whole family was there when the doctors said gravely that he would need brain surgery. Kaelan was conscious and listening alongside us. The light in his sparkly blue eyes dimmed when the doctor mentioned that his long hair would need to be shaved on one side of his head.

The day I showed up for *Survivor: Heroes vs. Villains* pre-game press was the day of his operation. My eyes were swollen from crying and drinking and not sleeping. I threw on a dress, brushed my greasy hair, plastered makeup on my puffy face, and let my razzle-dazzle fawn response lead me through the junket. The game had begun, after all. The whole cast was there, and I knew I was being watched. *Better look strong, Parv,* I thought. Any sign of weakness from this point on would be the death of me. I smiled through gritted teeth.

Kaelan's surgery went well and he was recovering in the hospital, scheduled to get sixteen staples removed from his head the day my plane took off for Samoa. I made a deal with the producers to notify me if anything happened with him while I was playing the game. They agreed, and I put on my game face, clear that I wouldn't speak of what I'd been going through at home to any of my cast mates. That kind of vulnerability was too dangerous.

When I competed on *Heroes vs. Villains* in the old-school era of *Survivor,* the game was the game, and contestants were characters for audiences to root for or jeer at. For my entire life, I'd prided myself on being strong and brave. I played that entire season with the recent horrors of my friend's brother's death and my own brother's traumatic accident weighing heavily on my mind. Still, I managed to play boldly: taking risks and winning challenges all the way through. And yet, when I found myself at that final tribal council, listening to Candice and Amanda and the others lay into me, I couldn't make sense of how I had cowered and stayed silent. I *was* strong, but hearing their words, I became frozen with shame.

When *Heroes vs. Villains* was over, I spent the fourteen-hour flight home feeling broken and isolated. I didn't want to talk to Russell, the guy who'd played by my side but ruined my game at the end. I wished Amanda would talk to me, but she kept her headphones on and looked straight through me as she snuggled with JT. The people I'd had a hand in voting out did not respect my gameplay; they took it personally. Now that the game was over and the cameras had stopped rolling, I was invisible to them, someone they no longer had to acknowledge.

Long after I came home, the memory of that final tribal council stuck in my body. I felt ashamed that I hadn't stood up for myself. I let them say all those terrible things about me and I just took it. Why didn't I tell them to fuck off? Why didn't I get up and walk out? A stronger person would have done those things, I thought. I blamed myself.

This is something that commonly happens when we go into freeze states. Because our culture in the West is so focused on independence, demonstrating courage and achievement, it's extra shameful for us when we can't hack it. We internalize the victim mentality and blame ourselves for the abuse we endure.

Then we get stuck in a cycle of shame that begets more abuse, which begets more shame. This pattern keeps a strong grip on us, and it doesn't let go unless we face it, accept it, and heal. But that can be a tall order for those of us who grew up in a culture that elevates resilience and self-reliance. The internal monologue goes something like this: *Our problems aren't that big compared to other people's. What's wrong with me? I should be over this by now.* The hard truth is that we *can't* just get over it. When it comes to shame and trauma, time does not heal all wounds. Shame breeds isolation, which doesn't lend itself to healing. We want to hide the thing we're most ashamed of. In my case, I felt rejected and unlovable, like a real loser.

When the season eventually aired, it was strange to feel so far removed from the love that was being poured onto me from fans, production, and the network. They all raved about my strength and tenacity. I was their star. But because I was so deeply lost inside my frozen shame pit, there was nowhere for this love to land. I couldn't feel it, receive it, or own it. I was sure they were all wrong. I was a worthless bag of trash.

When the finale aired and Sandra was announced the winner, I did press with her and Russell the following day. The journalists continued the onslaught of criticism I'd faced from my peers on the jury.

"You know, I can't pronounce your name, so I'll just ignore you like everyone else did on the show," one TV journalist said to me during a panel interview. I shrunk in my seat between Russell and Sandra, too defeated to fight back.

But feeling small and helpless didn't match my public image, and therefore was unacceptable to me. So instead of allowing myself to feel and name my shame, question it or reach out for support, my reaction to my low self-worth was to *do more* to prove that I was worthy of respect and love. I would be such a "good person" that no one could ever say anything to make me feel small again. I'd show those assholes I was a winner. I'd take my power back.

From this place, I took action. Relentless, urgent action. I built an upscale wellness center on trendy Montana Avenue with my best friend and business partner, Erika. I threw all of my *Survivor* prize money from the game I'd won, hundreds of thousands of dollars, into the center. We remodeled the entire space—knocking out walls, adding hardwood floors, and purchasing a large infrared sauna, massage table, handmade drapes, and deluxe desks from Pottery Barn. While we were building out the space, I enrolled in a month-long immersive yoga teacher training program so I could teach classes at the center, too. I poured myself into work so I wouldn't have to feel any of the pain from the past year.

While all of this was happening, my mom called to tell me that my brother was having problems. He'd started abusing the painkillers he'd been given after his surgery; the severity of his head injury was making him act erratically. He was having wild mood swings, angrily storming out of the house, and rejecting any kind of help from my parents. A few months after Kaelan had returned home from the hospital, he'd spiraled into full-blown drug and alcohol addiction. My mom was calling me daily for emotional support. I had no idea how to help her, but I felt desperate to do something. So, in between interviewing potential Pilates teachers and directing movers to bring in large exercise equipment, I fielded Mom's calls and listened to her painful stories. I was completely exhausted, but I loved my family and wanted to help, so I always answered.

"We caught him throwing a drug party in the basement. He came home stoned and bloody from a bicycle accident. He was out of control and screaming at us. What should I do?" she pleaded.

I held my breath, constricted my chest, and offered her calm emotional space and advice. I had no experience with addiction and didn't really know what to tell her to do, but I offered up ideas anyway. I couldn't see at the time that I really needed my mother to give *me* some of the emotional support I was giving to *her.* I was a full-grown almost-thirty-year-old adult. I wasn't a child anymore, but Kaelan was, and his needs were urgent. I could take care of myself. I *had* to take care of myself because my mom was dealing with something way harder than the thing I was dealing with. I tried talking to Kaelan, but he was totally shut down. My sweet little brother seemed like a stranger to me.

I felt sad, scared, and overwhelmed, powerless to help my family.

And I was stuck.

Frozen in shame, and in deep denial about that shame, I

continued to perform "fine." I acted as though everything was okay and smiled—racing through the day, teaching, entertaining, selling packages to clients. When I'd get home at midnight, I'd zombie walk myself to bed, and then I'd do it all over again the next day.

I ran on fumes and adrenaline for a year and a half until I totally lost my capacity to regulate myself or make healthy choices. I became a swirling vortex of chaos, and I was sprinting to keep up. Alternating between flight and freeze, I'd push away any worried thoughts about my brother by staying busy, running around the center grabbing towels to stuff in the washer. When an inspector came in to talk about building code regulations I didn't understand, I'd run into the massage room and close the door, hiding in the dark—paralyzed by fear. Money was pouring out as fast as it was coming in from the wellness center, destabilizing me further. I was also teaching four or five classes a day: yoga, meditation, boxing, and trampoline.

To take the edge off, I developed my own addiction to the allure of sex and power games in my romantic relationships. I couldn't fathom allowing anyone to see how hideously ugly I felt inside, so emotional availability or authentic intimacy were off the table. I continued to choose dominating, controlling, selfish, and arrogant men; overpowering them made me high. It's only in looking back that I can see what I was doing. It was an unconscious mechanism of the deep shame I felt that I gravitated toward people who would treat me badly.

My body was not a safe place for me to dwell in, so I left it, again and again.

PART II

UNDOING

5

Hunger

In the dark times we must find the kind of wisdom that combines an understanding of the darkness and the light.

—MICHAEL MEADE, *Awakening the Soul*

"**P**overty! Why did you name your child *Poverty?*" people asked my mother months after we left the commune.

"Her name is 'Par-*vuh*-tee,'" Mom said. "It means 'little mother' in Sanskrit."

Hearing this growing up struck some deep part of me, imbuing me with a purpose and direction beyond my small self. Even though I was only ten years old, I knew I would most certainly become a mother someday. I was destined for it. I hadn't really ever wanted to be a bride or a wife, but I always knew I wanted to be a mother.

Sometimes I mined the internet for information about my name. Parvati, the Hindu goddess. Wife of Shiva, the Creator and Destroyer of the Universe, and mother of Ganesh, the elephant-headed god who brings good luck, she is said to be the embodiment of the divine feminine. Parvati performed intense disciplines like sitting amid bonfires on hot summer days, going without clothing in the winter snow, standing motionless on one foot for great lengths of time, and fasting for long periods, all to increase her own magnetism and to attract the attention of Lord Shiva, her beloved. When I think about the Parvati legends now, I am struck by how much they sound like my experiences on *Survivor.*

As I grew older, I moved through milestones: graduated college, relocated to Los Angeles, won *Survivor.* The wellness center in Santa Monica I later opened with my winnings took more money, time, and energy than I expected, and my best friend and business partner wasn't able to do the things she'd said she would to run it with me. I ended up overworking and exhausting my resources to depletion just to keep the doors open. I survived two years like this until I finally sold the business at a major loss. I had nothing left. I was devastated and disoriented. I felt like a total failure, adrift without purpose.

After that, I pretty much spun my wheels without any clear direction for my life for a couple years. I said tearful goodbyes to many of my friends who moved away from L.A. to start families of their own. My dating life was full of drama and excitement and devoid of emotional intimacy. I dated a series of men, bouncing from bad boy to bartender to famous

Hollywood director to anonymous vacation flings. All the while I was haunted by the definition of my name. I was living for no-strings situations so I could call the shots and keep myself "safe." But throughout all my messiness, the impulse to be a mom never left me.

When I turned thirty, it was like Cinderella's clock struck midnight and all I could think about was having a baby. It was an undeniable force, a push from inside me that felt a void—an empty space that needed to be filled urgently. A compulsion that said I needed to change everything I was doing and learn how to commit to a relationship. The instinct was a stern teacher looming over me, telling me how much I was messing up. "You're an impulsive, emotional disaster. Get yourself together," the impulse jeered.

I yearned to be pregnant, to feel a little human growing inside me. But sadly I couldn't wave a magic wand and *poof!* myself pregnant. I needed someone else to give me the thing I wanted—namely a man with semen, a decent job, and a desire to be a dad. My longing commingled with my fear that I might never find this man, forming an urgent anxiety in my chest. I understood what the Buddhists were talking about when they said attachment is the root of all suffering, but it seemed impossible to shake myself loose.

I remember walking into Starbucks one day and seeing a new mom bouncing a chubby, gurgling baby on her lap. My ovaries ached, and I felt jealous as I turned away and ordered my coffee. I wanted that life. My fierce hunger for a baby became my guiding star. I was looking to start a brand-new adventure, and none of my old maps would lead me where I wanted to go.

Though I had the utmost respect for single moms, I wasn't willing to be one; it sounded hard and lonely to go that route. I needed a partner, but I had doubts that I could find a man stronger than me, let alone a good one who would love me and want to have a family together. Plus, I was worried *Survivor* had tainted me. I knew how the public perceived me from playing *Survivor*—I was a man-eating slut, playing all the idiots who were naïve enough to trust me—certainly not marriage material. I was scared that I was damaged goods. I mean, what man would want a woman who called herself a "black widow" and blindsided all the unsuspecting fellas who were foolish enough to adore her? Outwardly, I projected confidence and sex appeal, but deeper down if I was real with myself, I felt unworthy of the love I desired.

"Slide over," I said, as I threw open the back passenger door of Aras's Prius. Aras was a former *Survivor* winner from a different season, and we were carpooling to play in a *Survivor* charity soccer tournament. I squeezed in next to John, another former *Survivor* contestant. He was painfully handsome, with broad shoulders, dark honey skin, and soulful brown puppy-dog eyes—the leading man you'd imagine from a romance novel. It kind of hurt to look at him. I was instantly drawn into his orbit. When we picked up Ozzy, my fellow contestant and finalist from *Survivor: Cook Islands,* John slid into the middle seat and spilled coffee on his baby-blue soccer shorts. His leg touched mine. "That's what I get for stopping for a latte before seven A.M.," he said, laughing as he cleaned himself up. His self-possession and cool confidence felt new to me. *Wait, could this be my guy?* Most *Survivor* contestants I'd met had me on a pedestal. Their nerves bored me. I always knew I could eat them alive. But not John; his self-assurance magnetized me. I had to actively fight my impulse to lay my head on his shoulder in the car all the way to the tournament.

The timing of our meet-cute felt like kismet. Before my biological clock had flipped to urgent, I'd been terrified of commitment, worried that locking myself in with one person would mean the loss of my freedom. But now, the immediacy in me was intense and undeniable. I know I'm not alone in this feeling. Not every woman experiences this, but many straight women who want children are told to hurry up and lock down a good man before our eggs shrivel up inside our geriatric thirty-five-year-old uteruses. If, like me, you pride yourself on your independence and calling your own shots, this mandate of "needing" someone else to fulfill a personal longing puts you in an uncomfortable position. I couldn't create the baby I wanted so badly on my own, and time—I was told—was not on my side. Many of us, me included, get a little crazy when we feel the walls closing in on us. Not the ideal position you'd want to be in when you're assessing partnership material.

I wrote a list of qualities I wanted in a man. I meditated on what it would feel like to be with my person. I was actively manifesting a relationship that would lead to a family. Now, with his blue shorts next to my tanned leg in the car, I felt a pull. John seemed like the perfect puzzle piece to fit my dream, and we fell into dating instantly.

John seemed to check all the boxes. He was a literal rocket scientist with boyish charm and dressed like an Italian surfer in expensive T-shirts and Vans sneakers. He was playful and affectionate. After we met in the carpool, he got my number, and we went on some sweet dinner dates. We frolicked around, barhopping in the evenings under the twinkling lights of Main Street. He lit up like a Christmas tree when he introduced me to his friends. He had a great circle of close relationships—people he'd known from high school and college. We'd all meet for happy hour, where we'd drink skinny, spicy margaritas, eat bowls of fresh guacamole and warm tortilla chips, and bounce around Venice, basking in the golden sunset. His people were funny, smart, successful, and welcomed me in with open arms. I felt held, accepted, and included in a community in a way I hadn't in years.

Then, there was his family. At the time I met John, my family was imploding in emotional chaos surrounding my brother's drug and alcohol addiction. My foundations were shaken, and my core was destabilized by the drama. Meanwhile, John's family offered a picture of perfection, complete with traditional gender roles that seemed easier than what I'd witnessed growing up—both of my parents working hard once they got us out of the ashram, consumed by the demands of establishing our new lives and survival as a family.

The first time I met them, John invited me to dinner at

their family home in Orange County. When I arrived, John's mother, Jill, a petite, bubbly, brown-skinned woman with a bouncy bob, beamed as she enthusiastically pulled me in for a hug. "Welcome! We are *so* happy to meet you!" she exclaimed in her South African accent. Entertaining guests was Jill's favorite pastime, and she was shining. Her life looked a lot easier than the one my own hard-working, bread-winning mother modeled for me. *Wouldn't it be nice to be a housewife who hosted dinner parties?* I suddenly wondered. The thought shocked me in its newness. But then again, everything about me was changing.

I was ushered into the living room, where candles burned softly and Latin music played from the speakers. John's mother had moved from South Africa to Brazil in her late teens, and I admired the brightly colored art from São Paulo on their walls. Someone handed me a cloth napkin and a small china plate on which to place the delicacies they'd prepared on a decadent charcuterie board. Spread before me were dates wrapped in prosciutto, Brazilian puff pastries with cheese in the center, apricots, almonds, crackers, cheeses, cured meats of all kinds, grapes, berries, and pears. By the time I was whisked to the couch and seated across from John's father, Jim, John's brother David had already opened a bottle of organic red wine and handed me a full stemless glass. Jim steered the conversation, and it flowed as smoothly and richly as the drinks.

"Now, Parvati, I'm pretending I know what the word 'ashram' means," Jim said. "Will you please explain?" The room erupted in laughter.

"Well, an ashram is a community where people share a similar belief system and work together to feed, educate, and support one another," I replied simply.

Both Jill and Jim had spent many years overseas and lived in Brazil for some time, so the stories they shared were boisterous, colorful, and worldly. My parents had traveled a bit through Europe as kids and my dad had once hitchhiked across the United States, but they'd mostly hunkered down in Georgia to raise us kids. Everything about the Finchers sparkled like stars over the night sea. Best of all, they *worshipped* me for my performance on *Survivor*. John hadn't won his season, so I was a real superstar. Truthfully, it gave me comfort and relief to be in this power position. Being with them felt like being invited inside a warm house after a long, icy winter, then covered with a blanket of love. By the end of the night, my mind had decided this surrogate family could offer me the strong roots I needed to find steady ground again. On top of it all, Jill seemed so happy. *Maybe I could be a dutiful wife and mother, after all.* I left in a daze, blinded by the light of hope for a new domestic dream.

The months went on mostly like this, but sometimes things John did confused me.

"Where are you?" I texted and called. We had scheduled a dinner date, and he was over an hour late to pick me up. Finally, two hours later, he sent me a casual message that didn't acknowledge his extreme lateness. "Hey, shortie. What's up?"

This happened occasionally, and every time I worried about him. These instances also made me feel devalued, like I didn't matter enough for him to shoot me a quick text or give me a call and let me know where he was or why he was running behind. But when I talked to other people, they tried to get me to see things from another angle.

"Parvati, why do you look so upset?" my friend Tommy asked.

I was lacing up my running shoes at the front door with tears in my eyes.

"John is doing some things that feel selfish and he doesn't apologize about them or make it better. I think I'm going to break up with him," I said sadly.

"Hmm . . . John seems like such a great guy and you really like him. Isn't your pattern with relationships ending them when things get hard? Didn't you say you want to work on commitment?" Tommy asked.

I sniffled a yes. He was not wrong.

"Why don't you see if he's willing to go to therapy? You've got nothing to lose. If he says yes, then you may be able to work these things out," Tommy suggested.

Tommy was happily married to my yoga teacher Kia. I'd been renting a room in their large house for about a year and spent lots of time with them. It seemed like the healthiest relationship I'd ever witnessed. He was also over a decade sober and had just written a book on recovery. I came to him with all my questions about Kaelan and he'd give me guidance and emotional support. He was my lifeline. When we're feeling lost, we look for the one who is the least uncertain. *Tommy knows more than me,* I thought. So, although John and I had only been dating a couple months, we went to a therapist.

Much like the doctor who'd brushed off Kaelan's first incident with alcohol poisoning that night in the ER, the therapist wrote off John's behavior as his Latin culture.

"Don't people from Brazil have a different relationship with time than Americans?" he'd said. *But John was born and raised in Orange County,* I thought.

The therapist told me that there would be differences in a relationship like this that I'd have to be willing to tolerate if I stayed in it. This sounded logical to me. My own relationship graveyard was littered with poor, impulsive decisions. *Maybe I am the problem.* Maybe my gut was off, and I needed to listen to some experts and implement their wisdom while I recalibrated my own. In this way, I let myself be talked out of my concerns. The higher authorities I placed my trust in assured me that these things occur with all couples, and they would go away in time as we matured in our relationship and learned better communication.

About a month later, all my doubts washed away when John showed his dependability and kindness. My brother's addiction had devolved in an extreme way and my parents were in despair. Hoping to get him into treatment, they decided to do an intervention. At the interventionist's request, John flew to Georgia to support me. When things went haywire and my brother ran away and didn't come back, we were terrified. John was a rock the entire time, holding steady, comforting me and my parents, assuring us it would be okay.

"Hey, I know you're scared. We're gonna find him.

Kaelan's going to be fine," he soothed while supporting my body in a warm bear hug.

I knew I could count on him in hard times—a quality that outweighed the smaller moments of selfishness I'd observed. He'd make a really good dad, I thought.

And on a deeper level, there was also some sense of safety and specialness I felt in being chosen by a man.

I thought about how growing up in the ashram, the Guru had her group of "chosen children"—the kids she'd taken from some of the marriages she'd arranged. They'd lived with her and were allowed access to Ma's inner chambers. To my five-year-old mind, they were the luckiest kids on the planet. They knew her secret knowledge and captured her attention. Though the reality for Ma's kids was primarily abuse and neglect—and I was the lucky one whose parents had not given her up—my kid logic told me that I was an outsider, not special enough to be chosen. So, later in my adult life, if a smart, handsome, charming man thought I was good enough to be his *one and only girlfriend* and wanted to claim me in front of his friends and family then that meant I must be lovable, right? It certainly *proved* I had some kind of value that others could see. At the very least, it aligned with my girlhood fantasy of being rescued by a handsome prince.

But about three months into our relationship, John, the rocket scientist, suddenly left his job. That wasn't part of my plan. I was worried.

"This is perfect!" he said enthusiastically. "I've always wanted to get my MBA at Columbia University. Would you move to New York City with me?" I'd never heard him talk about New York, so this was news to me. But he worked really hard to perfect his application, and a month later, it paid off with an acceptance letter.

". . . Okay?" I said, questioning his sincerity and my own willingness to make a cross-country move so suddenly. When he assured me that he was serious, I was excited and felt shaky. I was totally smitten with John, but I wasn't one hundred percent sure about our future. I was clear I didn't want a long-distance relationship. I negotiated with myself—if I stayed in L.A. I'd be ending things with us, and who knew if I'd meet anyone else I liked. I'd always wonder about what if I'd taken the leap and moved to New York. I felt pinned against a wall. Moving to NYC was the only way to find out for sure.

I leaned on my old college journalism degree for the first time in my life. I asked my CBS connections from *Survivor* to help me out, and I landed a job as the health editor for *CBS News*. This was exciting. After being cast on *Survivor*, I had dropped my old college dream of being a broadcast news anchor, but now life was giving me a new chance. *Isn't it wild how things come back around? Must be fate.* I still felt the need to absolve the guilt I carried from betraying my friends on *Survivor*. I wanted to prove that I was a good person and could be more than a "greedy, attention-seeking, slutty reality TV star" as the critics had called me. Taking a job at a reputable news organization meant I was a worldly, smart, responsible citizen who was contributing to real, meaningful things. Beyond that, I was also committed to a real, grown-up relationship that took work and effort. I was a bona fide *adult*. And now maybe

I'd be an NYC mom—strolling my baby around Central Park and suiting her up in fuzzy snow boots for the winter.

But my imagined NYC fairy-tale life didn't land in reality. I hated the noise, how the high buildings blotted out my beloved sky, and schlepping groceries home on the subway. The city felt like an assault on my fragile nervous system, making me jumpy. On top of that, I despised going into the office for my news gig. I knew that I was lucky to have gotten this job. It was a dream job for any journalist and I was privileged that my *Survivor* connections helped me beat out the others. But I was thrown back into the memory of my very first job out of college where going to the office felt like a prison sentence. I thought I would feel better in an office this time, with this special job. But I was used to roaming, moving my body around the world—and now I was a caged animal being forced to sit at a desk for hours on end.

After ten months, I quit, not knowing what was next for me. I was stressed. I didn't like not knowing where my next paycheck was coming from, but John wasn't worried. He always told me how impressive and capable I was. He was sure I'd land on my feet.

I felt lost, but at least I had my relationship. Even though things weren't perfect with us—we fought a lot—we also had fun and it was better than facing the unknown alone. The relationship was something I could depend on. Besides, I was still aching for a baby.

After John graduated from Columbia, he scored a great job working for Anheuser-Busch. They sent him on a business trip to London in November 2016, and John invited me to join him there. I remember it was the day after Donald Trump had been elected president of the United States. His victory felt like a personal attack on my value as a woman. I cried about it all the way through the seven-hour flight from JFK to Heathrow. My eyes were puffy when I checked in to the hotel. John was in the city for work and he joined me in the room after he'd finished his last meeting of the day.

"Hey, I heard there's a secret champagne bar in Queen's Park."

Queen's Park. Champagne. He knows me so well.

I smiled. "Sounds perfect."

It was dark by the time we climbed into the taxi to take us there. John seemed distracted, which annoyed me. *I've just flown all the way here, can't you give me some attention?*

I laid my head in his lap. "What are you thinking about? You seem like you're not here."

"Huh? Oh yeah, I'm just thinking about work," he replied.

"Okay, well, put it aside for the rest of the night and pay attention to me, please," I insisted, showing my irritation.

The taxi pulled to a stop at the entrance of the park and we hopped out. John led the way onto the dark sidewalk, taking us through the gates.

"Are you sure you know where you're going?" I noticed some shadowy figures up ahead and suddenly became very aware of our surroundings.

"Yeah, for sure, it's right up here," John said casually.

We walked a few steps farther, until John spun around and faced me, holding both of my hands in his.

He dropped to one knee.

I was stunned. I'd been expecting a proposal at some point, but the timing of this one was a real surprise.

He made some kind of speech that swirled together with the emotions coursing through me—hope, joy, love, excitement.

"Will you marry me?"

"Yes! Of course," I said happily, and he slid the ring on my finger.

"Take me somewhere with lights so I can see this ring!" I bubbled.

We got married in July of 2017 in a sweet ceremony in Boulder, Colorado, surrounded by dragonflies and twenty of our close friends and family. A few months later, back in New York, I took a pregnancy test alone in a dingy CVS bathroom. I couldn't wait to walk the whole block back to my house. *Holy shit!* I saw the pink stripe and exploded into fits of giggles and tears. Warm waves of relief and glee washed up my spine. I was going to be a mom.

The instant I knew that a little being was growing in my belly, everything inside me shifted. The decades I'd spent living in survival mode had made me hard and rough with myself—always demanding more of my body. But, if mother and baby were to survive this pregnancy, I would have to soften, let go and surrender to an intelligent force of creation that knew more than I did. I started touching my tummy with love and tenderness. For the first time in my life, this part of my body wasn't a place to be controlled, sucked in, or tightened.

I let my stomach loosen and hang freely. In the beginning I told very few people, so I walked around New York City with a tiny Mona Lisa smile at the edges of my lips. I had this magical secret. I began to speak lovingly to my baby. I told her how happy I was that she was with me, and that we were a team. I let her know that I would feed her and help her grow and take such good care of her. Once I made it past the first few months and my nausea and fatigue lightened, I was able to eat. My cravings mirrored the foods that comforted me in my own childhood—Kraft macaroni and cheese, Lucky Charms, s'mores, and ramen noodles—things I never allowed myself to indulge in as an adult. When John brought me decadent, sugary Blue Star donuts, I squealed in delight. Over the course of my pregnancy, the edges of my body softened. I rounded out, thickened up, and my thighs rubbed together. For the first time, I didn't restrict myself, I let myself have what I wanted. I let myself be full.

My survival no longer centered around how quickly I could flee a predator. The hallmark of survival is it's a defensive state. It's tight, controlled, and ever watchful, scanning for threats. It requires a lot of energy to keep up those kinds of defenses, energy my body needed to make a baby. If I didn't let go of my survival mode of operating, my baby might not grow in a healthy way. Previously, whenever I threw myself into the unknown, I armored up and prepared myself for battle—knowing I could dissociate or muscle my way through pretty much anything. This time, I had to take the armor off to allow a new process to unfold. Everything that mattered to me, having a healthy baby, was outside of my control and required a new way of relating to myself and life—a softer, more surrendered state, trusting that I was cared for by a benevolent universe. I had to drop my heavy shield and sword to carry the weight of new life.

Survival in pregnancy was all about the baby, and for her to thrive, I'd have to kill the person I was before. I felt an intimacy and closeness between death and birth. I'd have to release my maiden self to embody a whole new identity: mother.

This process of undoing occurred slowly and mercifully over the course of nine months. We moved back to Los Angeles to be closer to dear friends and family, John's parents in Orange County, and my sister in East L.A. I spent time alone, journaling, resting—and grieving. I mourned the loss of the single girl who flitted off to faraway countries without a second thought, who could drink coffee or wine all day without guilt or fear, the hot girl who was light on her feet. None of this was me anymore—and might never be again—so while my baby grew inside me I let my old self dissolve.

I was *so ready* for this, starving for a deeper, more meaningful life that connected me to a higher purpose. Until this moment, I'd been busy trying to fit myself into girl boss culture, hustling hard to figure out what to do with my life. I hadn't landed on any career that stuck and I had no vision for my future. I was hungry for spiritual connection, for meaning. I wanted to love something with all my heart and soul. The baby in my belly was a grounding force that connected me to my life and made me want to dig in. Something funny happened when I stopped engaging in the hustle: I realized that I was being more productive than I'd ever been before. I was literally sitting on my ass, producing. Rest as the ultimate productive activity—this was a paradigm shift for me.

While I shed my old skin, I also gained faith in a power greater than me. There was certainly a powerful intelligence that was supporting me to grow this baby. I didn't realize it then, but I was also planting seeds of self-love. Because my baby was *in me*, all the love I was directing to her was going *to me*. I started treating myself with kindness, and instead of dominating my body, I started listening to it in a new way. Now I let myself rest when I was tired and eat when I was hungry. I started to reclaim agency over my own care. I slowed way down, not for me, but for my baby. The self-love I was generating was powerful and stabilizing. It gave me strength from the inside, not a power that I had to prove by competing with or being better than anyone else. This power wasn't validated by anything outside of me. My body was doing it all for me. My body's intelligence and capacity made me feel good inside and helped to heal the shame I'd been holding from my perceived past mistakes. To support my baby, I had to shift out of survival mode and teach my body that it was safe to relax.

It was a revelation.

"Has anyone here heard the myth of the Descent of Inanna?" Britta asked, making piercing eye contact with me and each one of the other fifteen expectant mothers and our partners in the birthing class.

Clearly, no one knew what she was talking about.

"You are all about to journey down into the underworld, where you will completely lose everything you think makes you who you are. In this portal, your old self will die and you will emerge re-formed in a new way as an entirely new being," she said, smiling.

I was terrified, and it looked like the other pregnant moms were, too. We had a feral vibe, sweatpants-clad, wild-eyed, and wound tight. I wasn't sure what had prompted the other moms to join, but I'd enrolled in the childbirth class after watching the horrific scene in *The Handmaid's Tale* when June gives birth in an abandoned house *alone*. In the end, she battles through excruciating pain and blood loss to deliver her own baby. The ordeal was chilling and cinematic. I was freaking out, and I needed to know what to expect, realistically.

When a teacher from my yoga community suggested I look up famous Britta Bushnell, author of the book *Transformed by Birth*, I pounced on it. The two-day immersive weekend would give me some much-needed information to help calm my raging nerves.

Our group made a semicircle around the teacher at the front of the room. Some people were in regular chairs. I was sitting on a Back Jack on the floor next to my husband. It was the only space left available when we'd arrived—forty minutes late on account of a fight we had on the way over.

"John, please hurry! They said don't be late," I had yelled at him from the passenger seat of the car.

"Where is my white James Perse T-shirt?" he yelled back from inside the house.

"I don't know. Grab a different shirt. Let's go!" I responded, my heart rate rising.

"You always hide my shirts! You do laundry and I have no idea where you put them." He dug his heels in.

Wait, is he complaining that I do his laundry?

After a bit more back-and-forth, he finally threw his body in the driver's seat, fury rising from him like steam. Once we were both trapped in the car together, the argument snowballed into a screaming match that culminated in me demanding to be let out on the winding dirt road that led up to Britta's house in Topanga. It wasn't a feeling of safety with my husband that made me get back in the car to reach our final destination, it was my desperation to have support for my birthing experience. I was still fighting back tears when I pushed the door open to join the class late.

As Britta explained Inanna, the air in the room seemed to thicken and crackle with anticipation. Holding our attention captive, she continued her story.

"Inanna is the ancient Sumerian goddess of love, sensuality, fertility, procreation, and also of war. She had amassed wealth, power, and respect as a queen, and was determined to attend the funeral of her brother-in-law in the underworld— the land of death ruled by her sister Ereshkigal. She pounded on the gates of hell and demanded to be let in," she said. The room stirred.

Britta's gentle smile, multi-layered beaded necklaces, and long, soft blond hair contrasted with the intensity of the tale.

"She needed to go through seven doors to get to her sister's chambers in the innermost sanctum. Each time she was allowed in one door she was forced to remove one item of clothing or jewelry—symbols of her worldly power. Until finally, she stands in front of her sister naked and vulnerable. Powerless. Her sister then commands that Inanna be put to death and hung on a hook, where she hangs for three days after she's killed."

I'd never heard the myth and was struggling to clear my head from the earlier fight enough to hold on to the complicated names and strange storyline. *What does this have to do with giving birth?* Usually I'm a big fan of myths and legends. My childhood and subsequent yoga trainings were steeped in goddess literature, and I loved it. But right now, in my state of high anxiety, I needed some real-life, practical tips, please. Not this metaphorical woo-woo.

Britta continued, "After three days, Inanna is rescued by one of her guardians from the upper world. She's brought back to life and returns to the land of the living with a newfound knowledge and wisdom of death."

"This," she said emphatically, "is your journey into motherhood."

Holy fucking shit. It's worse than I thought.

I didn't know it then, but pregnancy marked the beginning of a deep process of metamorphosis.

In our culture we don't really celebrate invisible work. During pregnancy, I became acutely aware of the productive power of rest and letting go. I'd been running so fast for so long, forcing and pushing for things to happen, that this time of resting on the couch and bingeing *The Handmaid's Tale* and *Friday Night Lights* reset my frazzled nervous system. I didn't even know how exhausted I was until I stopped moving and let myself sit still. During this time, I heard the story of the Chinese bamboo forest. Bamboo germinates for five years without any visible growth. All of the work is happening underground, invisible to the human eye. Then in the fifth year, it all shoots up rapidly. There was so much going on beneath the surface for me. Places in my body that were soft and vulnerable—places I'd neglected and ignored—were being activated and strengthened. In a way I was being brought to life alongside the baby growing within me.

When I tuned in, I could sense that I wasn't alone. I had a partner in this process, and it wasn't my husband. He was gone a lot, taking long phone calls during the day and going out with friends at night. My baby was my teammate. She was helping me grow as I supported her growth. At the same time, I was also being initiated into a lineage of mothers who'd gone before me. The depth of connection I felt to women and mothers was mythic and profound. I was held like a Russian nesting doll with my tiny baby safe inside.

Sitting in the circle at Britta's house, I sensed that becoming a mother would be a true hero's journey. None of us in that room would ever be the same.

6

Lockdown

"**S**ay hello to your baby," my doctor said, gently placing the tiny creature on my bare chest. Emotion swelled within me; the room swirled as I felt her warm, soft skin. Her head nuzzled into me, and I exploded into tears. Tears of relief, tears of joy, tears of exhilaration—I'd been holding this dream for so long and now it was finally real. Through blurred vision, I took in the whole scene. My baby's peaceful smile, the doctor down below taking care of me, John grinning over us. *Pinch me. I'm in heaven.*

Before we moved back to Los Angeles from New York, John encouraged me to leave the hectic business consulting job I'd been traveling the country doing for two years; he promised he'd provide for us until I could work again after the baby was born. I felt cared for and grateful. When we got to L.A., we rented a little two-bedroom craftsman bungalow a block away from Venice Beach and began setting up the baby room. Being near the ocean soothed my soul in a way I didn't know I needed. But things were far from perfect. A few months after we moved in, John had a confrontation with a partner; he was fired without warning, and unexpectedly, we had no income. I was seven months pregnant and scared, but I was grateful my parents had showed me how to survive in my early years. So, like them, I took action. I hired a veteran life and business coach named Amber and paid her nine thousand dollars—my entire savings—for three months of her time to help me start my own coaching business. I had no money left, so this had to work. She suggested I enroll clients by offering free one-hour conversations and if it was a fit, I'd sign them up for three months of coaching for a few thousand dollars. Thankfully, people did sign up, and the work was fun— I was helping others and putting my highly developed people skills to good use. I was learning on the fly and crossing my fingers that this would become a viable business. On top of people saying yes, I was surprised by something else. I found that helping clients with their lives relieved some of my *own* anxiety. My problems shrunk as I supported others through theirs. Meanwhile, I begged John to find work any way he could. We needed more money than the little spurts I was bringing in with my new business, especially with a baby on the way. But he didn't seem to have any of his former motivation or ambition.

"Maybe you could drive for Lyft?" I suggested one night, remembering my dad had driven a taxi at one point to help provide for his wife and new daughter.

"How *dare* you say that?" John was enraged. "I have a seminal degree from Columbia University. Do you think I'm a LOSER? I would NEVER drive for Lyft!" he yelled in my face.

I stiffened and shut my mouth, shocked at his anger toward me. *If I want security, I guess I will need to provide it,* I thought.

I also wondered what could be going on with my husband. Was something inside him preventing him from showing up for us?

By some miracle of grace, John's company insurance still covered our hospital birth. I delivered our daughter at Saint John's in Santa Monica, in a room with massive windows that let the Southern California sunlight pour in. She was born the weekend before the Fourth of July, so that evening fireworks lit up the night sky. John and I watched from the window while our baby slept two feet away from my bed. We exclaimed that the sparkly celebrations were just for us.

The next day there was a knock on the door.

"What's your baby's name?" a woman with a clipboard asked.

John and I glanced at each other nervously.

"We don't know yet," I said.

"Well, you've got twenty minutes to decide," she announced as she spun on her heel and left the room.

I clicked open the notes app on my phone, where I'd been keeping a list of potential baby names.

"How about June?" I said.

"Nah."

"Ama?"

I had seen the word in a travel magazine on one of my consulting trips.

"The Ama are Japanese women who live near the sea and free dive for pearls, seafood, and abalone," I said to John. "They've been doing this for thousands of years. They can hold their breath for over two minutes and some dive wearing just a loincloth and dagger. They're like real-life mermaids. How cool is that?"

"Yes! That's it. Her name is Ama," John agreed.

I beamed. We'd named our baby with ease. We were working together as a team in a way we hadn't before. I was hopeful it would continue this way. The family I'd dreamed of was finally mine.

But when I got home a couple days later, things changed. Back in my own house, without the support of the hospital staff, I couldn't ignore reality: It was all on me. I felt trapped—trapped in my home and in my body—beholden to this six-pound eight-ounce dictator. I became a fiercely protective, guilt-ridden, anxious, obsessive food bag, serving at the incessant cries of my newborn. I was also deeply infatuated with this tiny, fragile creature who was so completely dependent on me. Never in my life had I been so needed. It terrified me, and it gave me purpose.

Like many new mothers, I had the hardest time letting go of my girl. If I left the house for ten minutes, my thoughts would race. *Is my baby crying? Does she need me? I'm sure she needs me.* My body would brace, preparing for a call that would send me sprinting back home. Staying out of the house for an hour caused extreme guilt. *I'm a bad mom. I should be with my baby right now. She needs me.* An hour and a half and my tits would fill with milk and harden up like the protective bra I used to wear for boxing matches—you could knock on them like a door. I was on the clock and my minutes of freedom were fast ticking by. Two hours and milk seeped through my bra, soaking my shirt. Why didn't anyone tell me about this? As someone who bucked routine and schedules of all kinds, *I felt insane.*

I had no ability to classify what I was feeling at the time. I felt like there was a wild animal inside my body clawing at my rib cage anytime Ama cried, but I had only heard about post-partum depression. This wasn't that, but what was it? I knew something was off with me, but I didn't feel depressed. If anything, I was hyperactive, hypervigilant, hyper-attuned to any sound or smell that seemed off. My survival instincts kicked in and I leaned back on my old strategy—disconnect from hard feelings and just muscle through the pain. I may not have known entirely how to mother, but I definitely knew how to *survive.*

The motherhood template I'd been given by my own mom activated without me having to think about it. Though I hadn't been conscious of the way my mother had done things when I was a baby, she was my primary model. When I was born, she had been existing in the turbulent environment of the Ranch, responding to constant stress and fear. That imprint was in me and my nervous system whether I was aware of it or not. Remembering *The Body Keeps the Score,* I wondered, *Could that have something to do with the intensity I am feeling now?* The force was something I could not name—there was an animalistic protectiveness prowling inside me. It was like universal software programming of "Mother" had been lying dormant in my system for all these years and rumbled into life as soon as my baby was on the outside. Something beyond me had control over me.

It wasn't until years later, during the pandemic when my child was two years old, that I'd meet a mom on the beach who named the thing I could not. "Anytime my baby cried, I'd jump out of my skin. I was so terrified she'd suffocate in her sleep that I stood by her crib all night and watched her," the woman told me. "I was relieved when the doctor diagnosed me with postpartum anxiety. I started working with a therapist who helped me see that my hypervigilance wasn't me being a 'good mom,'" she'd said.

"Wait. Postpartum anxiety?" The phrase clicked for me. "I've never heard of that, but that is one hundred percent what was going on with me for the first year or two of my baby's life." I was floored.

It's hard to survive something you can't define. In naming the thing that had been controlling me, causing me to act in ways I didn't recognize or like, I regained some power. The act of naming something and claiming it can pull us out of isolation and fear. When we have a thing that's defined—something we can research and learn about, we can get a handle on it. It becomes just one part of us, not something that takes over completely. When we know what we're dealing with, we can join support groups, make connections with others, and share our stories. It was such a relief to hear that other new moms had the same experience as I did, and that they had made it to the other side.

But that revelation on the beach with the other mom wouldn't come for another couple of years. Back with my new baby in our Venice Beach bungalow, I still had a long way to go before I would get there. Mothering through the newborn phase made playing *Survivor* look easy. The mind meld of sleepless nights seemed never-ending. I had to remind myself repeatedly: *I wanted this. I prayed for this. This is my choice. It is my dream.*

At six months, Ama was finally sleeping through the night. Any breastfeeding mother knows this is a double-edged sword. We're so desperate for our babies to sleep, but our boobs take longer to catch up with the new development. Mine were still dutifully doing their job, filling up every few hours, prodding me awake like a cattle driver with electric zaps and drenched T-shirts. This was the state of my sleep-deprived existence when CBS called.

"Parvati! Congratulations on the baby," they said.

"Thanks," I replied warily, one eye on my baby, who was jumping up and down in her bouncy chair. *The girl never stops moving,* I marveled.

Even in my new parenting daze, I'd gotten hints of *Survivor* season forty being an all-winners season. I was certain I would never play *Survivor* again, but I had said if they did a winners season I could be convinced. Well . . . here it was, hitting me in my hazy, neurotic state. This phase of motherhood had me feeling like a trash can on the side of the road, getting picked up by a garbage truck with its big metal prongs. It squeezed and tipped me over its wide, open gulf, dumping the last of my precious insides and carrying them off to some junkyard, wherever they go. Obviously I would play *Survivor* again. But in the back of my mind, I knew it would take whatever was left of me.

During this time, my husband was making some choices I didn't understand. I'd expected him to see how much I was giving and roll his sleeves up to help. Occasionally he did, but other times he skipped town for ski trips and surfed with his friends.

"This is a strange time to pick up surfing, isn't it? I need your help," I'd said. "Are you sure you're not avoiding us?"

"Babe, I've always wanted to learn how to surf, and now we live in Venice. It's perfect timing," John replied.

The timing could not be more off, I thought, but I kept my mouth shut. I knew how quickly things could devolve into a full-blown screaming match, and I didn't want to expend my precious energetic or emotional resources on that.

When Ama was three months old, I asked my dad to come stay with me for a few weeks while John jetted off to Argentina on vacation with *his* dad. His trip came out of nowhere, and once again, the timing of it was confusing to me. John still wasn't working, and I thought his time would be better spent job-hunting than globe-trotting. I brought it up, but he shut me down, insisting it was a rare father-son bonding opportunity. I felt angry and unsupported, but I didn't have the clarity or problem-solving capacity to do anything about it. *Maybe it's a phase and he'll grow into his role of father over time*, I rationalized to myself.

While John enjoyed a leisurely pace, for me, time was always running short. I agreed to go back and play *Survivor* season forty, ultimately, because we needed the money. But I also wanted to be there for this momentous season of all winners. *Survivor* had been a huge part of my life for over a decade, and it felt like a kind of dysfunctional family reunion I could not miss. I had a few short months to stop breastfeeding, get my body into competition shape, and clear the cobwebs from my overwhelmed mind. This, on top of being the primary caretaker of my baby and building my new life-coaching business, sucked all the time out of my days and nights. I was a robot on autopilot; there was no time to feel or think deeply about what I'd agreed to do. The softness and rest of pregnancy seemed a long-lost dream. I was back in the familiar swirl of survival, armored up, focused only on what was just in front of me, and managing chaos like a champ.

To get into game mode, I needed to know that Ama would be fully taken care of when I was away. Since John wasn't working, he agreed to move with me and Ama to Georgia temporarily so we could be close to my parents for the time I was away filming. I found a full-time nanny and an apartment and paid for everything up front. After I'd set up my family, I hit the gym. Training wasn't so easy this time. I'd stopped breastfeeding earlier than I'd planned because I couldn't risk mastitis while I was away. My friend Ethan, another *Survivor* alum, joked that I should have just kept at it and I could have played the role of "provider" on the island. I laughed, but in the back of my mind, I was scared. I hadn't worked out in a strenuous way in nearly two years, since becoming pregnant. Would I be able to hack it this time? Or would I be a cliché— the out-of-shape mom archetype they love to highlight on the show. I really wanted to show the fans (and myself) that I could be strong even now, but I was gasping for air after ten minutes on the stair climber. Things weren't looking good.

The day I left my ten-month-old in her dad's arms at the airport, I was gutted. But I also felt excited. I was going to do the thing that made me *me*. I could step out of my new, all-consuming "mom" role and be "Parvati from *Survivor*" again! With butterflies in my belly, I walked through the sliding doors, spinning around to take one last look at my husband and my baby girl.

"What do I feed her?" John yelled from the car.

"That's not a funny joke!" I quipped back, praying it really was a joke.

Playing season forty brought me to the Edge, and that's not a metaphor. At all hours of the day and night, tears flooded my eyes—I was really missing my daughter. The game was hard and fast. I was voted out early on and sent to the "Edge of Extinction," where we had to trek up a giant mountain to collect a handful of rice each day to share with a growing number of mouths as more people were voted out and joined us. The Edge was a twist that involved booted contestants withering away in the hot sun and occasionally competing in grueling physical challenges to potentially win a coveted spot back in the game. We could tap out by hoisting a flag, but most of us had way too much pride for that. I spent the remainder of my time there trying unsuccessfully to get back in the game. When the game ended, my postpartum body had shed fifteen pounds.

I returned to the United States on my daughter's first birthday, a tweaky shell of my former self. I knew what it was like coming home after *Survivor*, but this time was different. I couldn't focus solely on rebuilding myself. I was still a new mom with a baby to care for. I needed support in my recovery, so Ama, John, and I decided to stay in Georgia with my parents for a while. My mom and dad had both become increasingly concerned about my well-being.

My mom and I circled the parking lot for a fourth time. We were heading to an Indian restaurant in Ponce City Market my husband had scouted and was raving about. Did I mention I was starving? And again, this was our *fourth* circle around the parking lot with no spots in sight.

I could feel the intensity welling up inside me, tightening my chest and neck. *I'm gonna snap.* From the corner of my eye, I spotted a blinker! The car to our left was about to pull out. *Hallelujah!* I thought. *We're saved!*

My mom threw her tiny Nissan Leaf in reverse and started to back up the few inches needed to allow the other car to reverse out of the parking spot.

HOOOOOONNNNKKKK!

I whipped my head around. A massive black Chevy Silverado was on our ass. I poked my head out of the window.

"Back up, please!" I shouted.

The car didn't move.

"I'm just going to do another lap," my mom said. She was not interested in a parking lot conflict and was getting visibly twitchy.

"No," I commanded. "Stay put."

Since returning from this last stint on the island, I had a hair-trigger response to stress. It didn't take much to set me off into a full-blown rage. As a consummate people-pleaser/peacekeeper, this behavior was highly unusual for me. But ever since I'd brought my baby home from the hospital, I'd been experiencing the most intense urgency inside my body. My normal daily anxiety and hypervigilance had ratcheted up about ten million times and I needed to respond to *everything immediately*.

Unsurprisingly, playing *Survivor* in this state didn't help balance me out.

I'd returned from the grueling game physically, mentally, and emotionally taxed, expecting to have some time and space to recover. I thought my husband would understand that I had just done something extremely strenuous and dysregulating for my body and nervous system. I assumed he'd jump into action, taking the baby out for walks and park hangs, maybe cook me some nourishing food. I thought staying with my parents would take some of the pressure off, and he'd have time to find work. But I was wrong, and I was fuming.

Earlier that morning, at six A.M., I'd left my sleeping husband in our bed and dragged myself upstairs to collect my crying child from her crib. I'd made her breakfast, fed her, and cleaned up. Around ten A.M., my husband emerged from the bedroom groggily, rubbing sleep from his eyes, finding Ama and I playing on the floor with some toys.

"Aggh!" he'd screamed and started hopping around on one foot.

"What?" I asked, unimpressed.

"I just stepped on dog pee." He was annoyed.

Whatever. I was unfazed. My parents had a very old black Pomeranian named Chester who could no longer control his bladder. He typically wore a diaper around the house, but I guess someone forgot to put it on that morning.

John went to the bathroom and washed off his foot. Then he sauntered over to the couch and flicked on the TV, leaving the puddle of pee right where he'd stepped on it. Cue my rage.

"Are you *not* going to clean that up?" I hissed at him through gritted teeth.

His eyes darted in my direction as if to say, *Are you talking to me?* "It's not my dog!" he retorted. The muscles of my neck tensed. Didn't he see what I'd been doing all morning while he was sleeping? What I was *still* doing now?

Smoke was practically seeping from my ears.

"You're a guest in this house. Clean that up, please," I said as calmly as I could.

My parents were super generous with their support, but living in an active senior community for over-fifty-year-olds in suburban Georgia didn't feel like home to me or my husband. We were both out of sorts and didn't have the skill set or capacity to regulate ourselves or communicate back to connection. The tension in the house had been mounting for days. I could tell my mom was worried about me. Growing up, I always tended to avoid conflict in favor of keeping the peace, but my long fuse and immense patience were running out. I was a stick of dynamite.

And now in the parking lot, I was a *starving* stick of dynamite.

I jumped out of our clown car and stormed over to the bully in the truck. "Hi, we've been circling the lot for a while now and this is our spot," I pleaded. "I need you to back up so we can get in it."

"I'm not going anywhere," the man sneered. He had reinforcements—another dude in the front with shaggy hair and a red trucker hat.

Who does this fuckface think he is? This spot belongs to me.

"Move, bitch!" a woman's voice yelled from the backseat.

I stomped to the front of the massive truck and planted my feet on the ground directly facing the grille that reached up to my waist. *If they wanted me to move, they'd have to run me over.*

My mom sped off, leaving me solo in my hostage-taking situation. I remained. Unmoved. The car attempting to leave the spot started gingerly inching out. It pulled an Austin Powers multi-point reverse to liberate itself from the tightest spot between my body and the other cars beside it.

Everyone was inconvenienced. I did not care. I was in full

survival fight response, seeing red. *If I'm not getting this parking spot, these assholes in the truck sure as shit won't either.*

HONNNNNNNKKKK!

The space was now free and clear. The man was screaming obscenities and threats out the window at me. With a crazed grin on my face, I motioned for another car to please help herself to this very free parking spot. Once the other car was securely in the spot, I spun on my heel and walked away. Throwing up a middle finger behind me.

I found my mom in the back of the lot, beside herself. "Parv! What were you thinking? They're going to key our car!" she said, alarmed.

"They are not going to key our car, Mom. Let's go eat," I sizzled.

I had so much repressed anger built up from the past year and a half that it felt good to blow off steam in this way, but something inside me told me this was not healthy. My anger had everything to do with my frazzled nervous system and how alone I felt inside my marriage. My operating system was stuck on survival 24/7. If I stopped working and taking care of everything, life would fall apart. John and I went to therapy, but things didn't improve. All the responsibility continued to fall on my worn-out shoulders. There was no time for rest, no time to recover, no time to process or think through how to resolve any of this pressure. It all just kept building behind the dam I was holding up to keep the pieces of my life in place.

We left my parents' house in Georgia and moved back to L.A. in December 2019. *Survivor: Winners at War* aired a couple of months later, in February 2020. I was still on autopilot, going through the motions, playing my parts: Mother, Reality TV Contestant, Wife, Life Coach. Coincidentally, on March 11, 2020, the day after Sandra—my old nemesis from *Heroes vs. Villains*—and I were voted out of the game in a double elimination episode, the entire world shut down as Covid-19 protocols locked us all inside our houses. With nowhere to run to and the pressure already at an all-time high inside my home, I was really freaking out. So I did what many people do when they're trapped; I escaped into fantasy.

"God, I wish we had met in New York. We were both living there at the same time. What could have been . . ." I sat alone in my car as I sent a wistful DM to the hot, sensitive, emotionally attuned man I'd been flirting with over Instagram since lockdown had begun a few weeks ago. His feed felt like a vacation to me; it highlighted beautiful places he'd visited, sweet pics of his dog, and more recently his hot lockdown lumberjack workouts. The man had just built a contraption to make maple syrup. He seemed kind and handy—so manly. I was feeling deeply alone in my marriage, and I'd given up on things getting better; the lumberjack was a welcome breath of fresh, pine-scented air.

"From what I know about you, you're not the kind of girl who gives up on something you want," he messaged back provocatively.

Wait a minute. Time screeched to a halt while I sat in my car alone with his message open on my phone. *Can I actually let myself go along with this new romance?* I was married. It was against the rules to get emotionally swept away with another man. What if I fell in love with him? *He lives in Vermont, Parv. You can't even go inside the grocery store, let alone hop on a plane across the country. You're also married?* I convinced myself that this was a good play, a safe choice. The pandemic created a natural barrier to this becoming a full-fledged affair.

I was on the brink in my marriage anyway—feeling like I was being held against my will inside an agreement or contract that was too tight and there was no room for renegotiation. I could barely breathe. My rib cage constricted like I was wearing heavy metal armor, only allowing the tiniest sips of air into my upper chest. With John, I couldn't express myself truthfully without things escalating into an argument, and I had been dancing on eggshells for months. I'd compressed myself into the tiniest little box way back in my chest. The smaller I was, the safer. I'd packed myself away and had adjusted to my minuscule container. I wasn't truly aware of how badly I needed an escape, an emotional release. The pandemic and ensuing closures of *all* my safe spaces had intensified the pressure inside and outside.

I didn't realize that I'd completely numbed myself to fit into the confines of my marriage until I started engaging with Lumberjack. He was interesting, building things, playing outdoors, and happy. He asked me questions about myself:

"How are you feeling today?"

"Tell me something about you. What was your childhood like?"

"What are your top three favorite books? Movies?"

I answered, hungry to share myself and be seen by someone who showed interest. We pinged messages back and forth daily. He sent me playlists of songs he liked. While my husband watched TV in the living room, I plugged in my earbuds and drowned out the scene around me, escaping into the sensuality and passion of Lumberjack's music. The sounds and vibrations mingled with my fantasies of being with this man across the country. I didn't need any of it to be real, I only needed to feel like it was a bit forbidden and *all mine*. *My* passion and sexual energy flowing through *my* skin. I felt a little guilty, but I'd had enough of sharing myself and my resources: my body and emotional energy with my baby, my money and my time with my husband—even my peanut butter with my *Survivor* colleagues. I wanted my body to be mine. I wanted this pleasure all for me. I wanted to play with the sensations inside me that were making me feel *alive* in a way I hadn't felt for years.

I marvel at the paradoxes of life, how we can find freedom inside confinement. And within our own minds. When I gave myself permission to lean into the flirtation, nothing outside of me changed. Los Angeles was under strict lockdown. Playgrounds were covered in caution tape and heavy chains. The beach was being patrolled by cop cars, anyone on the sand was aggressively scolded and sent home. I kept myself and everyone else safe by staying within the grounds of my two-bedroom duplex. My external environment stayed the same, relentlessly. But, inside me, Eros—the energy of desire—blossomed. My heart opened wide with new life, gratitude, and power. Instead of fleeing or clamping down on my body like my habitual survival responses would have me do, I spent time with my eyes closed, floating in deep meditation, feeling the blissful sensations that my flirtation with Lumberjack had awakened in me. During a terrifying pandemic where the primary collective emotion was fear, I felt the opposite—warmth, radiant like the sun. I felt Big Love.

I didn't know what to do with all this energy inside me. It was awakened by a man, but there was no path to developing a real-life relationship with him. So, was this about him at all? Or was it about me? I didn't care to figure it out. My body was bathing in the juicy freedom of love flowing through my veins. It was enough just to feel it.

At the same time, all over the world, people were streaming old seasons of *Survivor.* Just as I had felt trapped and found an escape through fantasy—globally, people locked inside their homes were finding their own escape fantasy through this adventure show. I think that because we were sequestered indoors with no end in sight, it helped to hook into something that showed other people suffering and surviving something hard. *Survivor* also hit another sweet spot; we couldn't travel or socialize, and the show gave us a sense of both, combining the beauty of a sunny tropical island paradise with compelling social gameplay. I related it to an episode of *Couples' Therapy,* where therapist Orna Guralnik talked about the real, powerful benefits of using an "escape fantasy" as a survival tool. Escapism provides temporary relief from the problems and stressors of the real world and offers our hardworking nervous systems a much-needed break.

The pandemic swept the world with fear, and lockdown

removed our typical coping mechanisms. For many, watching *Survivor* became self-care, a therapeutic tool that gave people a mental vacation from the horrors of the pandemic. People were longing for a sense of adventure, to feel excitement, to be in the action, even if they were only sitting on their couches. They were bingeing every season of *Survivor,* one after another, and talking about it with their friends; feeling like they were out there, playing the game, feeling the profound emotional responses of living on a deserted island, competing for a million dollars. The stakes were high, and the characters were complex. Escaping into fantasy can help us with emotional connection that can lead to catharsis and the ability to process and release our pent-up emotions. Something we all desperately needed in the pandemic.

New waves of fans followed me on social media and enrolled in my online coaching courses. They gushed about my game-winning strategy. Fashion-forward, trendsetting groups of gay men called me "Mother" for being an unapologetically flirty feminist. Love was returning to my life like an IV infusion; I was hooked up to a new supply. Their supportive messages helped bring back some of the positive self-regard I'd lost from believing the mean critics in the past. That, along with my emotional connection to Lumberjack relieved the sense of isolation that had grown from continuously biting my tongue in my marriage.

But on Memorial Day 2020, the door slammed abruptly shut on my escape fantasy when John saw Lumberjack's messages. It was a tragedy of divine timing. I'd been messaging with him on Instagram when my friend Tommy FaceTimed me. John had a little-brother relationship with Tommy, and when he heard Tommy on the phone he came and grabbed it out of my hands, plopping on the couch to chat. I sat down next to him to continue my conversation. When Tommy abruptly hung up to answer another call, Instagram was still open and there were Lumberjack's messages staring us straight in the face. It was impossible to deny. I'd never been so caught. I ripped the phone out of John's hands and shoved it under the couch cushion, sitting on it like a guilty little kid hiding the evidence. It was the most awkward, tense five minutes of my life, until John realized he'd been betrayed. Then shit hit the fan.

In a poof of smoke, my dream of escaping into something new vanished. I didn't want to do it, but because I wasn't ready to let go of my long-cherished dream of having my own family, I ended the flirtation and blocked Lumberjack on Instagram. With renewed passion, I threw myself into trying to repair my marriage. I told myself if I worked hard enough, I could survive this period of loneliness, too.

7

The Gift of Grief

"**P**arv, call me when you have a minute," my mom's text read.

Crickets had begun to sound their nighttime alarm. It was getting dark at the Florida Panhandle Park and I was buckling Ama, now two years old, into her car seat, trying hard to remember what random assortment of items we had in the fridge that I could miraculously turn into dinner. The text jolted me. Something was off.

I hopped in the driver's seat, threw on my seatbelt, dialed my mom, and hit the road.

"Are you okay to talk?" she said.

I ignored her question. "Is it Kaelan?" I asked.

I was worried. I hadn't heard from my twenty-six-year-old brother in a month. Last I knew he was shacking up with his girlfriend in Toronto, but he was known to pull the rip cord on relationships without notice and go off on self-described "wild hobo adventures," hopping on trains and staying in squat houses when the mood struck. He'd been in and out of treatment centers for drug addiction since he was sixteen years old. Since then, my parents, my sister, and I lived on a live electrical wire—like anyone who loves an addict does—praying for a miracle of healing while simultaneously pushing away the terrible fear that one day his addiction would win.

"It is Kaelan. He overdosed. It was an accident," she said in a strained voice.

It had started pouring and the raindrops pelted the car windshield like bullets. I felt the wind get knocked out of me. My breath began heaving in my chest. I glanced in the rearview, and seeing my daughter made my heart squeeze involuntarily.

INHALE. EXHALE.

Oh my God.

"Are you sure?" I asked my mom, pleading with her. He had overdosed before and been brought back. But I knew the answer.

"No, Parv. He's gone."

My mind raced. Thoughts and questions swirled chaotically. I gripped the wheel, trying to steady myself.

The following day, I began to experience this strange, intense pain underneath my right armpit. It was a throbbing ache that wrapped around my back like a rope and tied in a big hard knot just underneath my right shoulder blade. I imagined my brother alone in a room, scared and dying with no one to help him. I felt helpless, my spirit crushed. It threw me into a state of shock, my body braced like I'd been in a car crash.

My little brother's death would be the hardest loss of my life.

It was November 2020, mid-pandemic. Like many people, we'd relocated. John's dream was to build out a Mercedes Sprinter Van so we could travel in it as a family. He didn't have the money to purchase it himself but said if I bought it he'd do all the building, and we could sell it later for a profit. After my Lumberjack betrayal, I felt like I owed him something. Plus, it had been over a year since he'd worked a job, so I was excited that he'd found something he was passionate about. I knew John was smart and capable. I believed him when he said that this would be a good investment for us. With my new online coaching courses booming, I had the money, so I agreed to finance it.

I'd been leaning on my go-to survival strategy: working nonstop, taking care of my daughter, staying buoyant and hopeful, above the surface—not letting myself feel too deeply. I survived by getting up and surfing the waves, staying positive, taking action, moving forward. *I'm okay, I got this*—that was my mantra. It beat within me like the rhythmic, reliable pounding of my own heart. *I'm okay. I'm okay. I'm okay.* If I let myself fall beneath the waves, if I let myself not be okay, I knew I would not survive. But despite my best efforts, the death of my brother sucked me under. His death felt like the death of me, too. I was drawn into this liminal place, a shadow world between life and death. I needed help if I was going to make it back into the land of the living.

I hungered to be near my family. The day after my mom's phone call, I shoved some clothes inside a suitcase, buckled Ama into her car seat, and drove our rental car up to my parents' house in Georgia. John stayed in Florida for another week to finish the van project and then met us in Georgia for Kaelan's memorial, which we held over Zoom. It was surreal seeing Kaelan's friends from middle and high school alongside his street friends from train-hopping all in their neat little Zoom boxes. My parents, sister, and I all sat on a couch together facing the TV. The digital memorial made it easier for everyone to join the service, but the screens made it feel impersonal. I wanted to hug all these people and cry with them. I wanted to hold their hands and have them sign a guest book and invite them to write stories about Kaelan in black ink that I could keep with me forever. I felt numb.

The following week, I flew with Ama back to L.A. John drove the van solo across the country and joined us at home a week later. The dream of van life was dead to me. Living out of suitcases and moving around constantly would only add to the chaos.

By the end of 2020, I was completely depleted. I couldn't think about even one more thing. I begged my husband, "Please handle rent and bills for the next two months. I gave you most of our money for the van build, and I can't work in this state. I can't support other people right now. I can barely speak."

He hugged me. "I will, I promise," he said.

But when the first of January rolled around, John "didn't remember" that he'd promised me to pay rent. "I don't have the money," he texted. I felt deflated—and then, enraged. *If he can't show up for me now, in my darkest hour, this man will never be able to show up for me.* I leaned into all my survival strategies— fighting to stay alive like a warrior in the thickest, bloodiest battle. I pulled it all together, enrolled some new coaching clients, and paid the rent. But after that crisis was averted, another thought anchored inside me: *I've got to get out of this marriage.*

Like my parents, who one day knew they needed to get out of the commune, I was playing out a parallel dynamic. When I thought about it, my relationship felt vaguely culty. *Can it be called a cult if there's only one person in it?* I looked up the signs of how to know you're in a cult and found a list that included: absolute authority with no accountability, zero tolerance of criticism or questioning, financial nondisclosure, no justifiable reason for people to leave, a belief that the leader is right all the time . . . the list went on, and it sounded a lot like my marriage.

A few days later, I found myself staring at my computer again—the cursor blinking accusingly. I had just finished typing "how to get divorced" into the Google search bar. I felt like one of those people who notices a strange rash and flies onto WebMD to see all the terrifying things it could mean. I knew I was opening Pandora's box, but I needed information. Most of my friends were married, and I only knew two people who'd gone through a divorce. I breathed a heavy sigh. *Am I really doing this?* Yeah, my marriage was hard, but in a way, I knew what to expect. Kind of like my parents, who'd returned to the Ranch with me as a baby. The devil you know . . . right? Divorce was an unknown frontier, fraught with extraordinary loss, pain, and expense, and that made it seem even scarier. My anxious thoughts were interrupted by a text from John.

"Call me when you can," the message read. My stomach dropped. I thought back to a similar text my mom had sent me a couple of months before, alerting me about Kaelan. Bad news. John had been to the doctor for a colonoscopy and was waiting for test results. Immediately, I called.

"I have cancer. Stage four," he said.

"No, that's not possible," I said, confused. "Stage four is really advanced. You've been feeling okay. Are they sure?" I was shocked.

"They said I need to start chemo right away and will have to schedule surgery to remove the cancer." He communicated all of this matter-of-factly, like he was reading an article in the newspaper. He was acting strong, but I could tell that underneath, he was probably quaking.

I hung up the phone, reeling. *How could this be?*

Instantly, I was catapulted back into the role of caretaker I'd been desperate to escape. I shifted out of divorce research and into cancer care, reaching out to John's friends and setting up meal trains, securing good health insurance to cover his treatment. I called my friend Ethan, who'd survived cancer twice. He recommended some people to talk to and a support group that would pair John with a mentor who was further down the line with treatment and could offer guidance. It was nonstop phone calls and organizing, filling out paperwork and doctors' appointments. I was doing all of this while also trying to show tenderness to a man I was really angry with. Nothing felt real to me. The pain under my armpit intensified, as if my body held a megaphone yelling at me: *Girl, slow down! Feel this; you need to cry.* But I couldn't cry. Crying was a human thing, and I felt wispy, like a ghost.

The whole ordeal felt like whiplash. It had only been two months since my brother's death. And here I was, back again, suspended in a state of survival. I didn't want to stay in my marriage, but I didn't want my husband to die either.

I'm okay. I got this, I repeated, going back to my mantra. I fought back against my body's alarm bells, numbing myself like I was under some kind of government brainwashing. I couldn't let go, even if I wanted to. There wasn't time. I didn't dare let myself feel the depth of my sadness inside the house with my husband. His diagnosis took up all the space. There was no room for my grief.

I was cycling through all of my survival modes, pulling out all the stops: freezing sometimes from the shock of all the overwhelming events; racing around on Zoom calls with private and group coaching clients; speaking with health insurance agents; jumping on my Peloton to ride off the intermittent rage I felt flooding through me. Fighting hard to gain the upper hand with adversaries both external and in my own psyche. Fawning to get better treatment and answers from doctors, charming my way into securing daycare for Ama, tiptoeing around John's erratic moods. I felt fluttery and anxious, like a frantic canary battering herself against her cage. But even though I felt frayed, my survival modes kept me and my family alive, and I was grateful for them.

My flight mode helped me plunge into action, calling John's friends to set up emotional support for him while I doubled down on my coaching practice, enrolling new groups of clients. We needed money, now more than ever, to help cover healthcare expenses on top of paying the rent and bills. Although the single biggest pain point in my marriage was that John hadn't been working consistently, he certainly wasn't going to get a job now. I felt overwhelmed and resentful. I also felt guilty for feeling angry at John and for not wanting to take care of him. What kind of person resents someone who just got diagnosed with a life-threatening illness? *Only a real villain,* I thought. Still, I wanted out. Needed out. I needed space to breathe—to be alone and take care of *me.* My body was sending me SOS signals daily.

In response to his diagnosis and my avoidant behavior, John's survival fight template activated, too. He was ready to do battle with his illness and anything else that felt out of his control. He gripped tighter and tighter. There was no breathing room for any of us. The fights between us were loud and scary. We had a small guesthouse in our backyard. I worked with my clients out there and started to spend nights on the pullout sofa, too. Ama would come in to play with me, and I often drew oracle cards for us from my Wild Kuan Yin deck. One day I drew a card that read, *The slave girl dances to freedom.* That one struck something in me, a latent sense of: I want that. *Freedom.* That's what I want.

The chains of obligation and guilt were heavy around my ankles and wrists. In May, about five months after his diagnosis, I couldn't pretend anymore; I finally told John that I no longer wanted to be married. "But," I said, "as long as it feels safe, I will stay to support you through this." Though he hadn't taken care of me in my dark days, I felt a sense of wifely duty to help him through his cancer treatment.

But the tension between us intensified until it became insurmountable in August. It was my anger over the particulars of our marriage that finally helped me break free. It gave me the power to overcome my fear and filled me with energy to act. I knew then that staying in my marriage would mean letting a part of myself die—the part of me that longed for real, honest love and partnership. If I stayed, I would *never* know love. But if I left, at least I'd have a chance. It wasn't a guarantee, but a chance was enough for me. To fully live, I had to kill the dream I held so dear: my dream of a loving nuclear family with this man. I didn't care how much money it would cost me or how scary the process would be. I needed *the possibility* of real, honest love in my life. I hired a lawyer and paid his retainer fee that day, officially filing for divorce on August 21, 2021.

Next, I had to get the hell out of that house. I hunted for an apartment daily for a full month. I was turned down six times until one stuck. *Thank God I had some money tucked away. It would be nearly impossible for someone with less resources.*

After I found my new place, my sister, Sodashi, and my kind new neighbor, Trey, helped me move the few things I cared about keeping. Together, we piled things into Trey's pickup truck. I had been doing everything myself for so long that their generous support felt revolutionary to me. The new apartment was small, a tiny two-bedroom bungalow with a little side yard on a hill in Santa Monica. A large gate with a keypad to enter made me feel protected in a way I hadn't in years. At night, before I fell asleep, I thought of my brother. Though I couldn't locate him in the world, I could sense him near me sometimes.

Nearly a full year after Kaelan passed away, his in-person funeral was scheduled for October 2021. He'd be buried in Colebrook, New Hampshire, the tiny town my dad grew up in. The week that I was scheduled to fly with Ama to the funeral, John came down with some mystery swelling and landed in the ICU. His friend, a surgeon, told me, "This is it, Parv. Make sure Ama is around to say her goodbyes. John's not gonna make it."

I was rocked by the Sophie's choice of it all. If I chose to bury my little brother that would mean potentially leaving John to die while Ama and I were gone. If I stayed in L.A. to be there for John's final moments, I'd miss burying my little brother. I cackled maniacally at the intensity of the situation. It wasn't easy, but I chose to fly to New Hampshire for the funeral. And, miraculously, John got better.

Once I'd created a safe perimeter around me and my daughter, something new emerged from within me. It was a deep, tender sadness that had been packed away under my armpit and in my shoulder blade. It was the sadness I felt from years of hurting and suppressing my grief. When it was safe to feel—when my daughter was away at school and I was alone in my house—the tears poured out of me like buckets of water as those knots softened in my body.

For months, it seemed the tears would never end. My move marked a two-year period of transformation, coinciding with Kaelan's passing and leaving my marriage. Losing my brother changed the game for me. My trademark strengths that had helped me through *Survivor* and early motherhood—stoicism, enduring pain, self-sacrifice, dissociating—wouldn't work in this new landscape. I needed to shift my attention away from surviving and onto something different: healing and rebuilding. Navigating the process of un-learning my survival behavior, removing my armor, made me feel incredibly vulnerable. I felt like a baby deer with wobbly legs trying to stand and take its first steps.

I was on my own for the first time in a decade, and away from the chaos of John. I could finally feel my own energy and hear my own thoughts. Only then could I see how I'd been unconsciously creating the craziness in my life—my survival programming had kept me stuck in it. It was familiar chaos. Because I'd been afraid to feel my past and present pain, I'd been avoiding it by overworking, sacrificing myself, and trying to do everything on my own. In my own space, I sensed there must be something beyond surviving, and I was determined to find out what that was. I needed to reprogram myself to a new operating system—a whole different way of being and behaving in the world.

A few months after Kaelan's funeral, I filled my tub with Epsom salts and essential oils and submerged myself, dipping my head below the surface so the water covered my ears. I held my breath and let myself go under. *I'm not okay*, I wailed, pressing myself up and gasping for breath.

Memories of my brother floated up from the depths. I saw him at five years old making mischief at my high school graduation. His sparkly blue eyes and vibrant energy made him impossible to ignore. My sister and I pulling him in and smooching his chubby cheeks on his ninth birthday while he made a crazy face and rolled his eyes.

I sobbed for that little boy.

I wanted him back.

Twelve-year-old Kaelan at my *Survivor: Micronesia* finale, cracking me up in the front row because he refused to take off his sunglasses in the theater. When Jeff announced that I won, I ran down and hugged my whole family, pinching Kaelan and giggling with him about his cool shades.

"Congrats, Parv," he'd said through a shy smile.

"I love you, Kaelan," I'd said and beamed at him.

Later, my family and some of the other *Survivor* contestants piled into the elevator at the Dream Hotel for a party on the rooftop. The elevator got stuck between floors and my claustrophobia had me panicking. Kaelan, completely serene, glanced up at me. "Are you crying?" he teased. Some fire-fighters pried the doors open and I could finally breathe again.

The memories jumbled over one another like clothes in the dryer. I remembered the last time I'd seen my brother. He'd been hopping on trains and hitchhiking down the West Coast. Ama was six months old, finally beginning to sleep through the night. I'd gotten a text from Kaelan: "Parv, I'm coming through L.A."

I ached to see my baby bro. I loved him with every ounce of my being. But his addiction had started to make him act tweaky. He'd been sleeping on the streets, panhandling, playing his ukulele for tips and doing hard drugs with other severe addicts. I was an anxious postpartum wreck, and it made me nervous to invite him to stay with us. But he was my little brother, and I wanted him to know that I loved him, and I'd always be there for him. So, I asked him to come.

When he arrived, I gave him a massive hug, holding my breath on account of his street stink. He hadn't showered in days and was on some kind of hair-washing protest. "If you're going to stay here, you've got to wash that hair," I insisted.

"If I wash my hair, people will think I'm soft," he argued.

"Kaelan, you cannot sit on my couch until you've bathed from head to toe and scrubbed your hair with shampoo and conditioner," I responded, not letting up.

"You look tired." His eyes twinkled mischievously.

He was right, and he knew it.

"Coming from you, I'll take that to heart," I said, twinkling back.

We got each other.

Back in the present moment, sitting in my Epsom salt bath, my whole body ached. My stomach seized up and convulsed, pushing heat toward my jaw and cheeks until the tears burst from my eyes. The grief was excruciating.

I got out of the tub and toweled off. My body felt fragile, like the gentlest breeze could knock me down. I crawled into bed, curled up into a ball, and pulled the covers tight around me. I could see the green leaves on the trees dancing lightly through my open windows. Outside the world was beautiful, bright and happy, alive with possibility. Strange, I thought, how the outside doesn't match the inside; things can look so different to how we feel. It seemed wrong. There was a party going on outside my door and I was cooped up in my room with the plague. I wanted thunderclouds and hailstorms. Something that made sense with what I was feeling inside.

As I lay in bed, I sunk into the discord. Nothing made sense anymore and something about that comforted me. When my brain let go of trying to figure everything out, my body could feel. I dropped into the feeling and noticed something. Sitting right next to the sadness was relief. Kaelan's addiction had such a hold on him, and I knew how much pain he was in. He wouldn't have to suffer anymore. My family was forced to let go of the hope we'd been holding. We didn't have to live in fear anymore. The worst had happened. And here we were. The thought was a tiny balm on my broken heart. My chest felt like a hammer had been taken to it over and over again. It was tender and sore. I softened into the agony of deep love, and my survival modes began to fall away.

I squeezed my eyes shut. I was dealing with multiple deaths at the same time. The grief from losing Kaelan commingled with the pain of the high-conflict divorce I was going through. The dream of saving my marriage and keeping my family intact—dead. The custody split meant I lost my daughter for two- to five-day stretches, and not being able to contact her wrecked me.

Over and over in my head I'd see this vision: I was walking through a gray, war-torn city. The buildings were crumbled to the foundation. I climbed over rubble, picking up rocks and throwing them aside, looking for anything worth salvaging, but finding nothing.

I hadn't done this before—let myself feel pain like this. My whole life, I'd been avoiding pain, powering through via fight, flight, freeze, fawn. My response to pain was to push through it, stay positive, keep hope alive. But everything I'd been hoping for—everything I'd been struggling to save—was over.

My grief had taken me on a journey into the underworld; the rules were different here. Like Inanna the mythic goddess from Britta's birthing class, I was stripped down to the bones, without any armor. Soft and exposed. Beaten down and tenderized by my pain. Grief didn't care about my survival, or my old coping mechanisms. It held me down under the waves and forced me to feel all the pain from all the love I had lost. It showed me the depth and ferocity of my love. *Maybe there is something beyond survival.*

Many days, I wanted to be held by Mother Earth. The

mountains made me feel small and looked after by something timeless and enduring. So, I'd drive the twisty road up to my favorite mountain to hike in L.A.—Westridge Trail. I could always count on its immediate, full views of the ocean and city skyline to give me instant perspective and fresh life. One particularly hard day I was feeling anxious and angry, spiraling internally. I stepped foot on the trailhead and pleaded for support from the Great Mother, Planet Earth encircling me.

"I am here for a shift. I need help feeling better. Let my heaviness and anger lift on this hike," I begged.

I reached into my pocket for my earbuds and became even more furious when I realized I'd left them at home. "Damn," I sulked. I kicked myself into gear, anyway, walking fast past the easy trail full of hikers to the steep side. I wanted to be alone, just me, my body and this mountain. I didn't want to see or talk to another living soul. As I climbed the first hill, I noticed a raven flying nearby. I smiled to myself, remembering what my friend Tommy had shared at my brother's memorial.

"Kaelan was the trickster archetype. This type of person is handsome, devilish, and loves a wicked joke. They are world walkers, not subscribing to the norms of culture. They find ways to live and enjoy life that befuddles most people who try to find success through the means the world has laid out," Tommy had said. That very morning, I'd pulled the raven card from my spirit deck. The raven, the symbol of the trickster, death, mystery, and magic.

The synchronicity had me in a fit of little giggles and melted away some of the rigidity of my anger. A bit of space opened up inside me for something new. I kept walking. To my amazement, the raven kept flying next to me. *This can't be my brother,* I thought. But a tiny little voice in the back of my mind whispered, *What if it could be?*

I decided to test the bird. I stopped looking at it and began running fast with my head down. When I glanced up again, the bird was there in the bush right next to me. I was fully laughing now. This must be my silly brother playing a symbolic bird prank on me. With this thought, peace and love washed over me. My overwhelming heaviness and anger, gone in a miraculous instant. I felt my trickster brother walking right beside me, and I started talking to him out loud.

"You think you're funny, don't you?" I said.

Yeah, his voice tinkled back, inside my head.

"I'm so glad you're here. I miss you a lot. I wish I could hug you," I cried.

Parv, I know. I'm sorry. I'll be here whenever you want to talk, he replied.

I felt him. I saw his blue eyes shining. He was with me. Just then a man walked by. I nodded to him and kept walking, tears in my eyes. All of a sudden, I heard a shout: "Kaelan!"

With a jolt, I spun around to see the man who'd just walked by facing my direction. A small black dog ran past me toward him.

"Is that the name of your dog?" I asked incredulously.

"Yeah, it's a Gaelic name," he replied.

"I know," I muttered more to myself than to him, "it's also my brother's."

I'm entirely convinced that there is a presence or force

that loves us and wants us to grow into our fullest potential here on Earth. This force is the same thing that informs the cycle of life, the relationship between trees and mushrooms, the thing that turns a caterpillar into a puddle of mush and then a beautiful butterfly. That intelligence exists in all of life, so of course it also exists inside of each one of us. Just like the flowers, it knows exactly how to help us grow. It whispers to us about our rightful place in the universe. It speaks only words of love and encouragement from the depths of our souls. Not everything the voice tells us is pleasant or comfortable. It's usually quite the opposite. The whispers nudge us toward moves we need to make, difficult conversations we need to have, relationships we need to end, careers we need to change so that we can become the butterflies we're here to be. The whispers of love will bring us directly to the edge of the cliff we're meant to jump off—and we tend to be very, very afraid of doing that.

Since experiencing the extreme bottom dropping out in my life, I've found it easier to move forward in faith—trusting that this force is on my side and will walk with me as I follow its guidance. It hasn't been easy, and many times I've attempted to negotiate with the voice, but in letting it win I've loosened the grip of fear and control that I once bowed down to.

Slowly, through my grief, it began to dawn on me that my new power would come from a much different place inside me. My power wouldn't come from defending or protecting myself against pain. It would come from opening to love and allowing pain to be a part of life. It would come through knowing that there is something more beyond what I can see. When I let go of the struggle—of trying to control or force things to go the way I want, that's when life can show me the beauty in its design.

The truth is, it is love that allows you to move beyond survival to a place where you can thrive, and any time you love wholly you must surrender to the possibility of loss. Softening and relinquishing control, remaining fluid, allows you to absorb the shock of impact better when tragedy strikes, so that you don't shatter like glass.

Grief widened my ability to access love and acceptance. With it, I knew I could handle heartbreak. The process of feeling the pain of my losses cleaned me out, destroying old, outmoded ways of behaving, and paved a path to a completely new power source for me.

At thirty-nine years old, I was done with surviving. Instead, I was ready to love.

PART III

REBUILDING

8

Love

Alone in my new space, I searched for the toolkit my dad had left behind after helping me set up my apartment.

"Every woman needs her own set of tools," he'd said. "This is a beginner's kit for you: It's got a hammer, nails, wrenches, a drill, and different sized drill bits. If you end up needing more than this, I can help you add to it later." Then he gave me one of his trademark hugs, long and silent. Soothing. Calming. I could feel his chest rising and falling with his breath like the ocean.

Now that he'd returned home, I was on the hunt. *Okay, where is that freaking hammer?* I rummaged through the overstuffed linen closet. Towels, sheets, and extra pillowcases were threatening to explode outward along with some of my daughter's toys and games. I crouched down low and dug around on the bottom shelf. "Aha!" I yelled, finally pulling out the hammer and a box of tiny gold nails. I felt like an Olympic athlete standing on the top podium. Ready to hang my art on the wall, all by myself.

My divorce was underway. John and I had agreed to a fifty-fifty timeshare with Ama. That meant, for two- or five-day stretches I would be on my own, something I never could have imagined when I became a mother. The very minute Ama was on the outside of me, it seemed like she wanted to crawl back in. As a baby and toddler, she'd glued herself to me, not allowing me to shower on my own, brush my teeth, or sit down for a moment to think of something other than her or her needs. Over time, my brain adapted by reorganizing my thoughts to center around linear, daily tasks and planning, scheduling, and preparing. My once creative brain that could synthesize esoteric concepts and connect big ideas could no longer grasp anything other than the mundane routine of childcare. My world had shrunk to an island of two. The togetherness continued through my move to the new place. Dreaded separations always brought on tears and clinging little hands I had to pry off my body one tiny finger at a time. Heartbreaking. Now, inside my new apartment on this particular Wednesday, it was the first time I'd been truly alone in years.

Hammer in hand triumphantly, I walked to the living room. I stared at the white space before me. *I can put anything I want on this wall.*

Anything. I. Want.

Just then it struck me: My dream of a family didn't *have* to die with marriage. It could still come true. Now, with this blank canvas in my life, I could create any kind of family I wanted. I might not have a partner, but I had *myself.* I took a moment to let the idea sink in—just as I was intentionally putting together my new home, I could also design my new family. A family didn't have to be made from blood or a marriage contract. It could be created by bringing together people who matched my values; showed up with kindness, humor, and authenticity; and wanted to belong to my little tribe. I could make my home a bubble, a refuge of love.

Feeling steady and open, I pulled the neon sign out of its cardboard container. I held it flat against the wall with one hand. It was light enough to keep steady while I decisively hammered it in place. Once it was secured, I bent down and plugged it in. Instantly my living room was flooded with bright pink light. I stepped back to take in the cursive lettering, reading the word I'd decided to commit my year to: LOVE.

I understood the power of words. They vibrated with energy and substance. Words built worlds. I remembered when I was still married, living in the back house, poised to dismantle a world of shared matrimony. I'd written vows to myself then:

The truth will set you free.
I am creating myself new inside of this.
I choose to stay engaged and present within this great challenge.
I will allow myself to change and I will accept the changes.
I am choosing to live a life free from resentment and free from overwhelm.

I am committed to discovering and honoring my boundaries.
I will give and say yes to the things that feel aligned and correct.
I will say no to things I do not want to give.
I will trust my inner guidance to show me the truth.
I will express the truth with love and compassion.
I trust that what I choose to give is enough.
I will allow others to have their own experiences and feelings and I will not make that mean anything about me.

My vows were anchoring then and pointed me toward a way out. The sheet of paper I had written them on was placed on a shelf where I could see it all the time. Like a compass for a sailor out in the dark blue ocean, the vows guided me through my daily choices and aligned my thoughts with the future destination I was determined to get to. At the time, those words were aspirational. I was riddled with resentment and completely overwhelmed with the prospects of divorce, moving out, and starting over. Guilt was another heavy boulder on my chest, and I'd been silencing myself for months to keep the peace. But I kept the vows on display anyway. I needed them to be real. I just knew that if I paid enough attention to them, I could make them true.

Now, years later in my new home, I didn't need to reference that old piece of paper anymore. I'd internalized those vows. Over time, it became easier and easier to say no to things I didn't want to do, set boundaries around my time and energy to protect my peace, and slow down to listen to my inner voice. I started to have a blast being more direct in my communication. Instead of being terrifying like it once was, saying no was becoming fun for me. I got a little hit of dopamine, a surge of strength every time I used that powerful little two-letter word. I was doing really well with my commitments to myself, and it was time to level up.

It was the start of 2022 when I'd chosen *love* as my operating principle for the year. The word contained so much inside it—a sense of tender self-care, heartfelt connecting with others, playfulness and patience with my daughter, compassion with my ex-husband, presence and deep listening with coaching clients. Love felt strong and big—bigger than me. Like my old vows, it wasn't something I embodied yet, but it was something to reach for. I tethered my life raft to that word and prioritized it in every activity and choice I made.

Now standing back to observe the full effect of my new neon sign, I smiled. It would serve as a daily reminder of my commitment. It was also a fresh start. My old neon sign from the house I'd lived in with my soon-to-be ex-husband had read, LET THERE BE LIGHT. Recently, the L had stopped working, so it only illuminated ET THERE BE LIGHT. Instead of trying to fix it, I took it as a sign to move on. I'd tossed it and ordered the pink cursive LOVE sign instead. Staring at the neon word on my wall, I felt the power of this seemingly small change. It fit perfectly in this new place and felt so right. Everything in the living room, including me, was bathed in the color, essence, and light of love. It felt like a blanket of protection and something to grow toward.

Amid the back-and-forth shuffle of custody exchanges, two distinct and separate lives had started to emerge for me:

one as a determined single mother, and another, less formed version of myself that felt harder to define or contain. In the stretches without my daughter, I became feral, beastly, wild. I let myself go, eating cereal or popcorn for dinner in my underwear, washing down the simple carbs with a glass of red wine. I lined up all my coaching clients on one day, so I could see three or four empty days in a row on my calendar—more open space for me to play with. In those unscheduled days, I became Circe in exile—a goddess luxuriously reclaiming pleasure—walking around my house naked, touching myself, or taking midday naps in my side yard in the sun. The Wood-lawn Cemetery was only two blocks away from my apartment, and I soothed myself with long walks in the graveyard—listening to music in my earbuds, laying down on the grass amid the tombstones, and digging my fingernails into the dirt. Still grieving the loss of my brother and now the additional pain of not being able to see my daughter all the time, I let my tears fall in the grass. It felt nice cuddling up with death. Cozy, almost. At home, when my grief arose without warning, I dropped to the living room floor howling in agony.

Then, once Friday or Monday afternoon appeared on the calendar, depending on whose weekend it was for our custody schedule, as if by magic, I pulled myself together. I washed my hair, put on my jeans, and smeared on some lip gloss. Presentable and responsible. I hopped in my car to pick up Ama from preschool. On the fifteen-minute drive, a metamorphosis occurred within me. My wild woman retreated, and a capable, left-brained, organized, emotionally contained domestic goddess took the wheel.

Back in my linear mom brain, I'd send a text message to Ama's teacher Vanessa letting her know I was en route to pick her up. Since the split with her father she'd been having a tough time with transitions, so the text would give Vanessa time to prepare Ama for my arrival. She'd wrap up any work she was doing and get her backpack ready.

When I got my girl back I smothered her in kisses, excited to share the plans I made for us while she was away in her other life. I couldn't help thinking she was only three years old, far too young to be this independent from her mother.

"I have a surprise for you!" I said as we pulled up in front of our house after I picked her up from preschool one day.

"What is it? Tell me!" Ama cried.

"I hung something up on the wall, and it's your favorite color."

She ran to the gate and punched in the code on the front door, which she'd memorized already. Her sharp intelligence amazed me. I chased after her when she let herself in. "It's *pink!*" she exclaimed, twirling around the living room under the neon light. "I love it!"

With love as my guiding force, my little house became a cozy nest. I was the mama bird, inviting friends over to share in the sweetness I was building—the family I was slowly and intentionally creating. I scheduled dinners every Monday with two incredible twentysomething single women named Olive and Ariel. Olive was one of my original coaching clients in Los Angeles in 2018, and we'd kept a strong connection since then. She'd recently moved from San Diego back up to L.A. and when she was looking for apartments, she'd stayed in the back house at my old place during the very early stages of my divorce. She was made of sunshine and fairy dust. Ariel was the daughter of a dear friend of mine, a Kellogg School of Management professor I'd collaborated with on a project. Ariel was a petite, effortlessly cool brunette with deep brown eyes. She and Ama looked like they could be real-life sisters. Ariel was also new to L.A., missing her family and looking to make some good friends. It was a match made in heaven.

The girls loved Ama like she was their little sister. They played games with her, had dance parties and did art and scavenger hunts while I whipped up tacos or pasta for us. I felt like they were all my daughters in a way. Those nights, we were a family of four. Sometimes my sister would come and we'd all smush together to fit at my tiny circular dining room table. A family of five.

Since love was my major theme, naturally, I threw a party for Valentine's Day celebrating love and our chosen family, inviting my single girlfriends plus Olive, Ariel, and Sodashi. Ama decorated the house, cutting out giant pink hearts from construction paper, drawing faces on them, and taping them up on every wall and door. She took her role as host very seriously, welcoming our guests, giving them a tour of the decor and offering each of them a pink heart-shaped cookie we'd baked. We crammed into the living room and boogied to "Higher Love" and "Good as Hell" on my single ladies' playlist. Love filled our little two-bedroom apartment, spilling out of the windows and doors onto bright green Astroturf in the tiny side yard. In the end, we sent everyone home with a small bouquet of flowers and full hearts.

When my daughter was with me, there was light in my life. I worked out of pure devotion for the family I wished for her and the future self I was creating. I focused on making our home a place where playfulness and fun were nonnegotiable. Things were messy when she was around—gingerbread cookie decorating and painting pictures became body art as she wiped colored frosting or a loaded paintbrush up and down her arms and on her cheeks. "Don't touch anything!" I'd laugh, scooping her up under her armpits and depositing her in the bathtub. Sometimes, if she was hungry for a snack after dinner, I'd give her a container of yogurt in the bathtub—making the whole endeavor a full-on body spa treatment.

On weekends, I'd buckle her into the bike seat behind me and we'd ride down the boardwalk in the Santa Monica sunshine. We'd meet up with friends at the beach park and do dinner out before riding home exhausted at sunset. She had bunk beds with a slide in her room, but she insisted on sleeping in bed with me. I'd cuddle with her, making up stories and singing lullabies in the dark until she fell asleep. And our house was full of music: We started school days with Whitney Houston dance parties and sing-alongs in the car. I laughed hard with my growing girl and encouraged all of our creative impulses.

Because I invested myself so fully in her when she was with me, her absence on transition days felt like whiplash.

Going from single mother mode with days full of hectic activity, back to single woman mode with blank days full of nothing, was abrupt and disorienting. I felt completely emptied out.

"Where did you get that chair?" my mom exclaimed through the speakerphone, noticing all the new things filling up my living room. She zeroed in on the white linen circular daybed I'd splurged on in a moment of late-night self-indulgence.

"The Instagram ads got me," I replied wryly. "I wanted something sturdy and soft to hold me while I watch TV by myself." I squeezed my jaw to fight back tears. "It's so hard when Ama isn't here."

"Oh, sweetie. I wish I could give you a hug," my mom said, trying to console me from afar.

She and my dad had moved to Winter Park, Colorado, and were living there full-time now. Since my brother's death, they'd lost their connection and desire to stay in Georgia. Plus, my dad wanted to be a ski instructor; he'd become completely obsessed with the minutia of downhill skiing. I think it was a way to recover some of the joy he'd had as a kid skiing in the mountains of New Hampshire.

"I know, but it's okay," I said. "It's kind of nice to be alone in the quiet anyway. This is the first time—*ever*—that I've lived alone. Maybe I need it to figure out my messed-up life on my own." I was doing my best to reassure her. I'd been doing this act with my mom since I was young, since we moved away from the Ranch and started over in Georgia. She had worked her fingers to the bone to set up our new life, and I'd vowed to myself then to never be a burden to her. With her, I was always "okay."

We said goodbye and I put my phone down on the cushion beside me. Sitting in the quiet stillness of my new apartment, I scanned my environment. There was my familiar green couch and my happy pink rug. The old me still in the mix; the new me taking shape. I felt gratitude and pride for what I'd created and a pang of longing for my child that was missing from the scene. Turning my face toward the light, I took in the bright sunshine pouring through the corner windows. Hummingbirds chased one another around the jacaranda and the big oak tree just behind them, standing tall and strong, its green leaves tinkling and shimmering in the gentle breeze. It was a perfect day in Southern California.

In the peace and quiet of my new space, I felt something I hadn't felt in a long time: boredom. I'd become so accustomed to chaos that the sense of calm sent me into some sort of excitement withdrawals.

I grabbed my phone impulsively, and flicked open a dating app I'd downloaded but hadn't done anything with yet. As a public person, I'd hesitated to put myself on dating apps, an arena dotted with potential land mines no matter your profile. I had the added concern of having been on reality TV. I certainly didn't want to date a *Survivor* fan who might have preconceived notions of who I was based on my performance from over a decade ago. I wondered if my history would continue to haunt me. But out of boredom and curiosity, I persevered. I whipped through my profile with little thought, giving just the basics: Single mom, thirty-nine years old, female, looking to date men. I wanted to see what was out there before I invested too much time writing something great to sell myself. I started swiping:

Dan, 38, marketing, no kids, no pets, loves fishing.

Rob, 41, banker, no kids, likes cooking.

Aaron, 37, firefighter, two kids, single dad.

Aaron looks okay, I thought. I swiped right.

That night I had a nightmare about leaving Ama at the playground alone in the dark because I had to meet a date. My subconscious was showing me I was not ready to get back into any kind of romantic relationship. Dating was a dark pit filled with spikes. Underneath my curiosity was a terror that I would create another relationship like the one I had recently left.

I remembered John saying something to me when we were married that made my blood boil. "I thought our life would look like this: I'm a powerful CEO, and you're my wife standing by my side, looking beautiful and charming the other executives—making me look good." He'd said it to me nonchalantly at the breakfast table one day, a couple of years into our marriage. By that point, the pandemic and our incredible financial strain had already started to drive a wedge between us. The frustrations piled up day after day. And then came this new revelation—that, all along, he wanted me to be some sort of trophy wife? I was *fuming*.

I dropped my spoon, splashing cereal milk on my white T-shirt. "Are you serious?" I glared at him. "If you'd painted this picture of your dream marriage when we were dating, I would have run for the hills," I said, my voice dripping with resentment.

"No need to get so intense about it," he said and laughed.

In that moment, it struck me, in quite a dramatic way: I had married the patriarchy—a system built upon using women to prop up the power of men. In becoming a wife to John, I'd stepped into a traditional and historic gender role and was expected to constrain myself to the code of ethics inherent within it. Based on how he was raised, he expected me to be the selfless mother of the family, putting his needs first, while bolstering his career and raising our child. I'd lost myself inside of that unspoken dream for a long time. I would not—could not—fall into that trap with another relationship. I couldn't play that role ever again.

Okay, so maybe dating would have to wait. I needed to understand myself more to make sure I'd choose a better match next time. But how? I barely recognized anything about myself anymore. With my daughter, I was a ceramist straddling the wheel, both hands holding steady while my bowl spun, capable, confident, controlled. I pushed, pulled, and smoothed the clay to make a full and round shape, a bowl big and strong enough to hold all of the things of her life. Without her, I let the wheel spin out of control. With both fists

I smashed the bowl, pressing it down so it held nothing, flat and sprawling. Destroying it with gusto. In this way, I wove back and forth between forms. And with each custody exchange, I reclaimed bits and pieces of myself, molding them, pressing parts of my soul back into my skin. I was an artist following the mysterious muse, creating a sculpture or a painting, with no sense of what it may become. I was an unknown creature to me.

Why did I enjoy strolling around in the graveyard and lying on the living room floor naked, surrounded by piles of unfolded laundry that I wouldn't touch for days? Why did I spin around in circles inside my house trying to make a plan for the day—putting clothes and sneakers on for a walk, opening my front door and promptly closing it to retreat to a bubble bath at eleven A.M.? I couldn't even decide what to eat for dinner when my daughter wasn't around.

What I really wanted, I thought, was someone to hold my head in their lap and stroke my hair while I cried, like I did for my child. Someone who could soothe me and tell me everything would be okay. A soft, gentle, and sturdy presence that I could relax into. I wanted someone who could take care of me.

I sensed that because I'd lost myself in my previous relationship, my comeback would require a whole new kind of relationship—one based on trust, mutual respect, and care. But I didn't trust myself to choose a good man for me, and I was too full of my own complex emotions and mothering my child to hold space for a partner's heart.

Maybe it wasn't a man I needed after all. Maybe, what I really needed was to be nurtured, to be mothered myself.

9

Body Language

"Stop!"

I barely had time to follow the screaming voice of my guide before my ATV took a nosedive over a steep sand cliff. Everything whipped by in a blur of beige sand and cloudless blue sky. My hands white-knuckled, gripping the handlebars for dear life. The bars twisted and my right arm stiffened and locked, bracing for impact. After the front of the four-wheeler hit the ground it rebounded, snapping my head backward and fracturing my right wrist.

Coming to a stop in a sandpit I froze. Shocked, I staggered off the bike. Thank God it didn't roll forward and crush me completely like I'd heard had happened to those German tourists who'd been riding around in these exact same Namibian dunes just weeks ago.

My body collapsed onto the hard sand, and I lost consciousness.

Ten years later, I lay covered in silver aluminum on a therapy table. My ATV crash while filming *Around the World for Free*, a TV show I was hosting for CBS where I was challenged to circumnavigate the world with no money, was long in the rearview mirror. However, inside this therapy office in the thick of my divorce and dismantling my old identity, covered in a silver aluminum blanket (the same kind paramedics give to people in the immediate aftermath of a shocking tragedy)— the memory came rushing back to me. Sara Pettit, the owner of the dance studio/therapy office where I was receiving treatment, was in her late sixties and resembled a Greek goddess with her close-cropped white-blond hair and a dancer's elegant frame. As an acupuncturist and somatic therapist, Sara would skillfully guide attention to her clients' bodies to release stored emotion, trauma, and tension. In doing so she'd bridge a healthy relationship between the body, mind, and nervous system.

In need of nurturing, with my own mother far away in Colorado, I'd enlisted Sara, along with a few other women healers and therapists I'd nicknamed "the mamas" to play surrogate mothers to me. Week by week, I'd show up in their offices and they would hold my head in their hands, prick me with needles, and dig their elbows deep into my fascia while I cried. They'd been through their own difficult trials and re-garded me with empathy, accepting and validating every vul-nerable emotion I shared. Allowing others to see me feeling anything but happiness was hard, a relic of my old survival persona. It was a smiling mask I'd carefully built upon the belief that showing emotion was vulnerable and would get me hurt. This aversion to vulnerability also had something to do with my hyper-independence—a conditioned, American cultural sense of duty to "do it all by myself." Plus, in my family, my parents had been so busy trying to carve out a life for us beyond scarcity that showing unpleasant emotions seemed like it would only add more weight to their already overloaded shoulders.

On Sara's table my eyes closed. Something a former yoga teacher had once said in class floated up from somewhere in my body's dark, cavernous intelligence: "Healing needs a witness." The mamas were giving me a safe space to feel the feelings I'd denied or repressed throughout my entire hyper-controlled life. Their gentle, consistent presence was helping me to make it okay to feel, and in turn, making my body a safe place to inhabit.

I was trying hard to relax on the table, but my body was not cooperating. It was shaking uncontrollably. "Good," Sara said in a calm voice. "Let that happen." I was grateful for the permission. I had no ability to stop the contortions anyway. My right arm began jerking forward and back wildly.

"Is there an image or memory coming to you?" she asked.

"I'm in Namibia about to crash my quad bike," I replied in a throaty whisper.

"What would you like to do?" she asked.

"I don't understand the question," I said back.

"If you could stop before the accident, would you want to do that?" she prompted.

"Yes."

"Go ahead and stop the bike," she said. "Press the brake and pull on the handlebars and stop it before you go over the hill."

I can stop? The thought had never occurred to me. I visualized and acted out slamming my right foot down on the brake and squeezed with both my hands. I felt the bike lurch and come to a halt just before the place where I would have flown off the cliff. The relief in my body was palpable. It felt like a complete reorganization within my system. I didn't have to keep racing toward a cliff. *I could stop.*

This was a revelation. Up to this point, I'd been in fast-forward. My flight response was always on, ready to pick me up and move me toward the next thing. I thought back to how my family had fled the commune. That may have been when this pattern solidified in me as a way of life—pick yourself up and move on, always be thinking of what's next. It's how I won *Survivor.* On the island, I barely slept. I'd lay awake at night anticipating my next move and thinking through options of how others would respond, watching the domino effect play out in my head before the light of dawn broke through the dark. Safety, for me, came from getting ahead of what was coming my way. Perhaps the greatest benefit of living this way was I didn't have to think deeply about anything that had hurt me in the past. I didn't have to remember the pain I'd caused my devoted college boyfriend Liam when I finally broke up with him for good. The times I'd abandoned myself and tolerated mistreatment, my brother's accident, his years of addiction and the worry that tortured my family. I didn't realize, however, that even while I kept going, pushing the past out of my mind, my body held on to the lived experience. I guess you can't outrun your past, after all.

Peter Levine, the founder of Somatic Experiencing (the type of bodywork Sara was performing on me) says that trauma happens in the body as well as in the mind:

> Trauma is something that goes on in the brain, but it also goes on in the body. Our body goes through a number of specific reactions to meet that threat. We duck, we dodge, we stiffen, we retract. We prepare to fight or flee, or we collapse into helplessness. These things are meant to be temporary. However, humans get stuck very often because they're not aware of what the body has done to respond to that threat, so they remain in that position. When the body is in that position, it tells the mind that there is danger.

My fast-paced lifestyle had never allowed me to fully process the trauma of my accident (or any other traumas I'd experienced for that matter). At the moment of the crash, fully immersed in my role of TV show host, I was so focused on performing—and so good at dissociating from my body—that I had barely allowed myself to accept that I'd been injured. After I regained consciousness, I simply picked myself up, dusted off my jeans, and kept smiling for the camera. My wrist surgery in Johannesburg was even woven into the show. I'd gritted my teeth and forced back tears, not wanting to appear weak.

Now that my whole life was unraveling, I *had* to look at where I'd been so I could create something very different for my future. In Sara's office, my body felt safe enough to let me relive that painful event of my past so I could transform it and release it. This was one of many traumas that had taken up residence inside my body. I'd experienced many things in my life that had overwhelmed my ability to cope in the moment. Times when my body's survival mechanisms mercifully kicked in, allowing me to dissociate so the pain wouldn't be unbearable. Apparently, those experiences were still very much alive inside me.

Levine says that Somatic Experiencing creates the context for the body to show us these stuck memories one small bit at a time so that we can release the threat response and restore our bodies to a place of safety. When we release the defensive posture, we can relax and find more ease in our lives. Then the world is a friendly place again. When Sara gave me permission to stop, to put my foot on the brake of that bike, I felt my body relax, unraveling some of the tightness it had been holding on to for so long.

When the session was completed, I opened my eyes.

"That was incredible," I said.

"Your body did some good work today." Sara grinned at me.

I walked out into the bright Southern California sunshine, taking in the expanse of cloudless blue sky above me. I got in my car and put it in drive, but before I moved forward, I paused and noticed. Something powerful had unlocked within me. The bracing tension that had come to feel so familiar had been replaced by a new and strange sensation: freedom and expansion in my chest. Lightness and space. My anxious, fluttery heart felt calm—for the first time, maybe, ever. I placed my hand on my chest, acknowledging my heart's presence. It responded with contentment, settling in deeper like a bird returning from a long journey—legs curled up, wings tucked into her sides, soft, round belly filling the nest. Landed.

Home.

Pressing my right foot down on the gas on the drive back to my apartment, I felt my car respond to the pressure and move forward. Pulling up to a stop sign I would normally roll through, I slowed to a full and complete stop. *I can stop.* The revelation continued to unfurl as my eyes absorbed the full scene: tall palm trees swaying in the breeze, vivid fuchsia bougainvillea flowers, green grass. *I can slow down.* I was in charge of time, not the other way around. My body had shifted out of the current of survival, threat, and urgency. I had dropped into flow—fully present and alive inside of this moment.

Sara's sessions and my other bodywork were helping me develop a true friendship with my body for the first time. I'd been disconnected from my body for so long that I felt clumsy in recognizing its signals, like a child learning a new language. I had to sound out my feelings, say things out loud to myself to connect sensation to information—information about where to go, what to eat, what to say yes to, what to avoid, and where to slow down so I could think things through. My body was becoming my wise companion and my guide.

The blue Pacific Ocean whizzed by on my left as I continued my drive home. Taking in the swirl of sand and sea, it became clear to me that I had some repair work to do with my body (like I would with a friend I'd hurt). I had to tell the truth about how I'd been my body's oppressor, controlling and forcing it to perform for me. How I'd hurt it, abandoned it, and judged it when it needed tenderness and care.

My body is a sovereign being with its own biology and needs. It's been there for me and loved me this whole time. My thoughts brought waves of sadness. My heart ached for all the years I'd spent in hostility toward myself. I grieved the lost time. But the body is a forgiving animal, bent toward love and programmed to heal. Grateful and relieved to be seen lovingly and accepted at long last, my cells opened up like flowers toward the warm sun. Tears flowed directly from my tissues, muscles, and bones, up and out through my eyes.

For months, I devoted myself to learning body language—working with Sara, my other healers, and my own personal practice. Thankfully, I had a bit of saved money in my account from my previous coaching workshops, so I didn't need to stress about enrolling new clients or leading programs. Slowing down in my business was unfamiliar to me, but I wanted to establish safety in my body so badly that I was willing to tolerate the discomfort of taking so much time off work.

I focused on healing like it was my full-time job. I did somatic therapy, craniosacral therapy, acupuncture, Rolfing (a form of specific deep tissue massage that helps release stress patterns from fascia or connective tissue), holotropic breathwork, and practiced yoga nidra (a form of meditation that involves deep rest).

Over time, I started noticing when my body braced itself—the sensation of tightness in my chest, the shallow breathing, a hard ball in my stomach, or my low back or hips stiffening up. I learned to identify these as little defensive relapses into survival mode, and they happened daily—often occurring alongside some fear of perceived danger or not having enough (time, money, space, love, etc.). With Sara and my other therapists' skillful guidance, I started connecting my body sensations to the thoughts in my mind that matched them. This was powerful Truth coming from inside me. I was learning who I truly was and how to be my own authority. I thought back to who I'd been: the little girl on the commune, the teen adapting to fit into a new urban landscape, the survivor, the wife, the mother. All these different roles and identities had come with so much uncertainty and self-doubt that had prevented me from holding myself with my own conviction. With this new awareness and understanding I could begin to write a new story for myself, and that included using my voice to set boundaries and ask for what I wanted.

During this same period of healing and re-learning, I met Cara, a fellow divorcée with two young children who lived in the Bay Area. We'd connected through a mutual friend named Anna who'd set up a WhatsApp group for single moms going through tough divorces. I didn't know many people in my situation, and I longed for an understanding community. Though we were spread out all over North America, the women in the group were a lifeline for me—especially Cara. She and I held similar beliefs around dating and sex, and now that we'd saddled back up in the Wild West of dating, she'd recommended the book *Existential Kink*, by Dr. Carolyn Elliott.

"Each of us has a dual nature: we are light (conscious) and dark (unconscious)," the book description reads. "The dark side of our personality—the 'other,' the shadow side—is made up of what we think is our primitive, primal, negative impulses—our 'existential kink.' Our existential kink also drives the dark or negative repeating patterns in our life: always choosing the abusive partner or boss, settling for less, thinking that we're undeserving, not worthy. But it also is the source of our greatest power."

After reading this, I instantly purchased and downloaded the audiobook. I had been struggling with the custody split between me and my now ex-husband, feeling the agonizing loss of my daughter. I'd done a ton of therapy to help me heal from the past and now I needed new mental constructs to support me through my present grief. I devoured the book in two days while walking around my neighborhood and in my car driving to pick up my daughter at preschool. It breathed some space in my brain for a new way of holding pain, a new way to be in my body.

One of my most powerful takeaways was the raunchy permission it gave me to own all the negative or mean things I'd believed about myself—or all the times I'd exploited myself or allowed myself to be used or mistreated. For so many years I'd been slut-shamed and called selfish and greedy when I was competing on *Survivor*. Remember the journalist who wrote: "I'm surprised it was the locals who taught Parvati how to catch crabs and not the other way around"? And when my fellow contestant Ozzy stood in front of me at the final tribal council in *Survivor: Micronesia* and asked me: "How does it feel to choose greed over friendship?" Through the lens of *Existential Kink*, instead of judging myself or any of that as wrong or bad, I could be more exploratory with the experience. I could ask myself about what part of me *liked* being promiscuous or taking what I wanted even if that meant someone else would lose out. This line of questioning felt abrasive at first, but as I sat with it a little longer, I found it liberating. It removed my resistance and judgment and allowed me to see myself as a more *whole person*—a blend of good and bad, moral and immoral, kind and cutthroat. It helped me accept myself in a deeper way.

Then, I got curious about how I could give these "slutty" and "greedy" parts of me what they wanted in a healthy way. I'm not saying I deserved to be shamed for how I behaved, nor am I granting permission to anyone to slut-shame others. However, when I applied existential kink to these painful past experiences, it felt right and empowering to claim these parts as *mine*. If a part of me could embrace the "slut" label for all that it entailed, then I didn't have to be a victim. I didn't have to, unconsciously and haphazardly, create drama in my life. If I wanted to play around with this aspect of myself, I could consider it in a thoughtful, deliberate, and safe way.

———

I was ready to experiment with the *Existential Kink* techniques in the real world—but first, I needed to find a play partner. "Do you know any good guys I could hook up with?" I whispered to my friend Hannah while our kids played a few feet away on a park bench.

"Oh, actually yes!" Hannah replied. "My former boss, he's a doctor. He just got divorced and I was telling him that he should start dating. I should set you up with him! Actually, hold on—" She winked at me, then quickly turned to her phone and put us all on a group text.

"Efficient!" I beamed.

Later that day The Doctor texted me. "Hi! I know I should wait a few days to text, but I have a free night tomorrow and want to see if you're available," he wrote. "I know I should say I'm busy, but I don't have my kid tomorrow night and I am free as a bird," I replied, thirsty.

We met up the following night at a lounge called Casa Del Mar. I slinked through the door feeling like Cat Woman in tight black jeans, a black bodysuit, and black stiletto lace booties. The Doctor was already seated on a couch waiting for me. He was cute, his white pants contrasting nicely with his smooth olive skin and kind brown eyes.

"I'm nervous," he said with a little giggle.

"That's sweet," I said. "I guess I am too, a little."

We each ordered a glass of prosecco and chatted about the usual first-date stuff. He asked about my family and where

I grew up. I asked about his kids and how he's been since his divorce. He told me he was remodeling his house now that his ex-wife had moved out. It felt good to claim the space and make it his own.

"Cheers to that!" I smiled.

The night wound down and he paid the check and walked me to my car. "I'm not sure if I should kiss you or not. How does it work on first dates?" he said shyly. I found him completely endearing, but I wasn't sure we had any sexual chemistry. I went for a hug, dodging the kiss.

"Can I take you out again?" he asked.

"Sure," I said, smiling. He was nice enough for another date, and maybe the attraction would grow. On date number two we went to dinner at a spot in Venice with live music and a disco ball. He opened up more about his life and his professional goals.

"I'm opening two new urgent care centers now. It's exhausting, but I know it will be great when they're up and running."

"You sound like a busy man. How do you possibly find the time for romance?" I asked playfully.

"Yeah, it's all work and taking care of the kids for me. I haven't dated in decades. Even when I was married, I barely saw my wife. Maybe that's why things didn't work out," he said with a laugh. I liked that he had a sense of humor and a bit of self-awareness. After dinner, we walked around the Venice boardwalk. It was dark, but one shop was lit up and blasting Latin music. The Doctor started dancing and I joined him. He held his hand out to me confidently. I took it and he twirled me around. *The man's got rhythm,* I noted to myself. Again, he walked me to my car. This time I let him kiss me, and the fireworks took my breath away. *Oh my god, he's a really good kisser. This will only get better from here.*

We slept together on our fourth date, and it became evident that The Doctor truly did have a healing touch, a gift. After that, I dubbed him "The Sex Doctor." Whenever I didn't have my daughter, I dashed over to his house, or he'd come to mine at all hours of the day and night for hookups. I'd shimmy in through his sliding bedroom door while his teenage kids slept in the other wing of the house and we'd have hot, fun sex. Afterward, I'd slide out the same door and drive home, preferring to sleep in my own bed. My body *loved* The Doctor. It was feeling more alive, appreciated, and cared for than it had in years. But while the sex was great, emotionally and mentally things just couldn't seem to line up with us. For the time being, though, that was okay with me; it was still early days in my divorce, and I didn't have the capacity to care deeply for anyone just yet.

The Doctor made a great playmate, and I was owning my slutty, greedy desires, and having the best time doing it. After about nine months of this, I wanted to up my Existential Kink factor. I got excited by the thought of bringing some of my more risqué desires to life in the bedroom. I wanted, for example, the thrill of being tied up and having to break free. I was clear I didn't want to feel victimized, trapped, or helpless in my daily life, but something about playing those parts in the bedroom turned me on. I emailed The Doctor about kinking up our sex. The email was an exercise in asking for what I wanted in a direct way, and seeing if I could find a way to create the tension and adrenaline I was seeking safely.

He responded with an enthusiastic "Yes!" and said he was excited to try out some of the things I'd asked for in my note. I felt elated.

But months went by, and The Doctor did nothing out of the ordinary. The sex was still off-the-charts good, but I started to feel annoyed by his lack of acting on my request. "Pick up some rope at the hardware store before you come over tonight," I prodded in a text one day, not quite ready to let my desires go. "I'll make sure to bring it. Can't wait to tie you up," he answered, delivering just the words I needed to hear.

When he arrived later empty-handed, I felt deflated. He knew how much I wanted this, and again, he didn't follow through. It had taken a lot for me to share my fantasies with him, and I needed him to make the next move as a show of his *own* vulnerability. I had to know that he could meet me in the unknown, that he was brave enough to do something different. I was throwing him a layup, all he had to do was dunk the ball. Plus, I was already taking care of so much in my life, giving so much: supporting my daughter and my clients, taking creative risks in my work, nurturing my friendships— I didn't want to "take care of this," too—especially after I had already explicitly told him what I wanted. And frankly, I had enough of doing it all myself, being strung along by men saying they would do something and then not keeping their word. Every time it happened, I felt small and insignificant, like my voice didn't matter. I also felt icky, thinking maybe he was just telling me what I wanted to hear to keep me on a hook, so I wouldn't leave.

After a few months, it became clear he wasn't going to follow through on his word, and I began to lose trust in him. The sex started to feel empty. It reminded me of how I felt in my marriage. As an experiment I stopped initiating meetups with him. This showed me something important: If I didn't text him, he didn't text me. After a week of not hearing from him, I asked him to call me. He texted hours later saying he missed my message. I called him and he didn't pick up. When he texted back the next morning, he said he'd fallen asleep. That was the end for me. I told him I wasn't interested in continuing what we were doing anymore; that it no longer felt right to me. It was new and empowering to communicate my boundary in such a clear, direct way.

I had been scared to completely shut the door on The Doctor. *Where would my fun come from now?* But then I remembered the words I read in *Good Chemistry* by Julie Holland, another book from my healing reading list: "You can never get enough of something that almost works." If I stayed in this situationship I'd be giving up something that I was starting to honor above all: my truth. My truth was, I was breaking free from the old conditioning that taught me desire was selfish and wrong. I wanted more, and that was a good thing. I needed to honor all parts of myself—the slutty, greedy parts alongside the generous, "good girl" parts—and I wanted to be with someone who could do the same. I needed to know that my voice was real and the things I said mattered. I wanted people in my life who would follow through on what they said they would do, people I could trust and rely on. I wanted a partner I could experiment and play with, someone who would value and match my creative impulses with openness. I'd been too brave and lost too much to settle for anything less than what I truly wanted anymore.

10

Beyond Binary

"**A**hahaha! I have a dick!" I looked down at my lower half and cackled.

The strap-on was boggling my mind. I'd always only seen myself as a seductive woman with all the tricks of a belly-dancing temple priestess. Ultra flirty femme. Mae was lying next to me on the bed, looking a little nervous about my big reaction.

I'd had lots of sex with men. I felt highly confident in my sexual prowess and capacity. It was always a fun game for me. The objective: Turn on the man by playing with the power dynamic. Become a siren, pulling him into my orbit with well-rehearsed moves, sounds, and sights. Then move away, forget about him, become engrossed in my own energy. Dance, giggle, and let him find me and pull me back in. It was so familiar.

But this? This. Was. Not. Familiar.

In my shady bedroom with the curtains drawn, I looked at the flesh-colored dick sticking out of my body where there had only ever been empty space. The cognitive dissonance instantly shattered my lifetime paradigm of how sex was "supposed" to go, and I was finding it hilarious. The bubble in my belly rose up and burst out of me in full-body laughter. Tears streamed from my eyes. The release was powerful. Then something clicked into place, and I looked at Mae.

"I'm going to fuck you with my dick." I smirked. It was their birthday, after all. Mae's bright blue eyes grew big and round. "Oh my Goddd." Their voice deepened with a mixture of turn-on and disbelief.

I met Mae at their comedy show in L.A. just over a month before. A strange, synchronistic series of events had unfolded, guiding us toward each other before we ever met in person. My sister, Sodashi, went to a show where Mae mentioned *Survivor*. She thought Mae was hilarious and because I was always up for a laugh, maybe I'd be into meeting them. So, my very supportive, curious sister googled "Mae Martin Parvati Shallow" to see if Mae was a fan of mine or if they backed Queen Sandra, my *Survivor* frenemy. She wanted to make sure the water was warm before she asked me to wade in. Sodashi's internet research returned a tweet Mae had made while living in England in 2020 at the time when *Survivor: Winners at War* was airing.

> I love Parvati and Boston Rob from *Survivor* so much that I just cried about it, but nobody in England knows what I'm talking about.

Coincidentally, a few days before my sister shared her intel with me, I'd gone on a date with a writer from *The Flight Attendant* and had just finished watching season two of the show. Mae was in it and played an ambiguous, villainous attendant named Grace St. James. I remember seeing them on screen and being intrigued. *What's this person about?* I wondered, like you would about any interesting character you see on TV. I wasn't thinking I'd ever actually meet them in person. But now that my sister brought the tweet to my attention, I couldn't resist sliding into Mae's DMs with a line of my own: "Heyy why haven't you invited me to one of your shows yet?"

Mae replied almost instantly saying I was invited to any show I wanted. I bought tickets right away. Strangely, two days later, my good friend and entertainment reporter Evan Ross Katz sent me a voice note saying he was interviewing Mae on his podcast and asked me to send in a question for them. It felt like a wink from the universe. I jumped into the current, sending the question. Then I promptly dove into Mae's comedy series *Feel Good* on Netflix. I needed to know more about them. I devoured two seasons in a weekend, and I still wanted more. The show was smart, funny, and so sexy. Mae was magnetic. The following day, the girl next to me at yoga had a tattoo on her forearm: the word *Mae*. I rubbed my eyes. Yep. It definitely said *Mae*. I approached the girl after class to make sure I wasn't hallucinating. When I asked her about it, she confirmed it was her grandmother's name.

Meeting Mae felt cosmically aligned with the new life I'd been carefully constructing, one of creativity, joy, and bold aliveness. The universe was holding out this glittering, rare gem of a person in a package that was completely new to me. I was crushing hard, and wide open to the possibility of this very new experience, before we locked eyes a week later at the comedy show. Afterward, I wrote in my journal: *They are absolutely beautiful and captivating and it felt good to be near them. I want more of that feeling—like I'm walking through a doorway out of a dark hall and into the light.*

I knew Mae was an absolute diamond, and I'd never wanted anyone so much. But I was still nervous the first time we hung out. I worried that Mae was in a different phase of life. They were fairly new to L.A. and focused on building their career in Hollywood. I was a single mom to a five-year-old, rebuilding my identity after a rough divorce. *Did Mae want me, too? Was this even a date?* These questions lingered in the back of my mind as Mae hopped in my car and I buzzed us to a bar in West Hollywood. On the way, Mae pulled out a notebook and started rattling off rapid-fire questions: "Blue or green? Hot or cold? Sub or dom?" I laughed. Mae seemed nervous, too. The questions sparked some lively conversation, and I loved how Mae listened deeply, interpreting me through my answers. I felt giddy and a little shy, like I'd never been on a date before.

At the bar, Mae told me they'd booked an escape room for us. "It's okay if you don't want to go, but I love escape rooms and it would be so fun to do one with you," they said. "Let's do it!" I replied enthusiastically. I wanted to play some more. The escape room was located in a strip mall in an obscure part of town I'd never visited. Mae's friend Kayla met us there. In the strange room, doing puzzles as fast as we could, I brushed Mae's hand and felt electricity. Our bodies kept finding each other in the dark. It felt like we were finally meeting again after spending lifetimes apart. The chemistry popped and fizzed between us. When I dropped Mae off at their place late that night, I was already head over heels. We've been inseparable ever since.

Back in bed, I was admiring my lover. Mae's a beautiful mix of boy and girl. Or neither, really. They're nonbinary, and they'd been with lots of straight women before. Only some of them ever want to wear the dick. This was an exploration for both of us—I'd only ever been with men before, and Mae knew this. Both of us dove into a field of infinite creative possibility, playing in the void together. It was exciting, making it all up in the moment.

Now that I had my new, manly appendage, the pressure I normally felt to perform my specific role of "woman" was gone. Freedom pulsed throughout my whole being. My heart flew open. I climbed on top of Mae and I pressed my dick into them, watching it go in and out. I gripped their short blond hair and pulled their head back toward the pillow, leaning down to kiss their mouth. I was actively, passionately present, wildly turned on inside this entirely new experience.

When did I internalize the idea of what it meant to be a "woman"? Was I five years old? Six? What limitations and tiny boxes have I been squeezing myself into to fit that definition since then? Who would I be if I let myself expand beyond all of that?

Thoughts and questions swirled around in orgasmic, cosmic clouds. I was happy. Dazed. Melted. I was not who I thought I was.

Afterward, we lingered in bed for a while, tangled up in each other's limbs, enjoying the afterglow. But responsibilities tugged our bodies out of bed. Mae had a birthday party on the East Side, and I had to pick up my daughter from school. We both needed coffee.

I drove us to Go Get Em Tiger, a little window coffee shop on Main Street in Santa Monica. Mae got a chai, and I ordered a cappuccino with oat milk. Everything outside looked the same, but internally my brain had been turned sideways inside my skull. There was a rift in my identity. It reminded me how I felt when I left my house for the first time after becoming a mother. This major thing had happened in my life, but everyone else was just acting normal. *Weird.*

We had an extra twenty minutes before we both had to be where we needed to be, so we went for a walk to the beach. I reached for Mae's hand and realized that I was now out in the world with this person who is not a man. With our fingers intertwined while we strolled, we looked very much like a couple. Just then, two twentysomething dudes holding skateboards walked toward us, and my stomach tightened. Would they say something to us? Would they attack us? I knew that people could be mean and sometimes violent toward people in queer relationships, and I had never been in one before. Were we safe?

Squeezing Mae's hand, I took a deep breath. I wondered if Mae could sense any of the things I was thinking. I stretched my head up toward the warm sun. My authentic desire was leading me off road, far away from any map I'd ever followed. I glanced at Mae, who didn't seem to notice the skateboarders or any of the internal questioning clanging around inside my head.

As the boys passed us, opposing thoughts rose up from the depths. *What is safe, anyway? Is it a big, strong man who would fight those guys for me? Or, is it someone who I trust to hold me steady in the midst of my fear? Someone who allows me to be myself, explore new territory, be vulnerable and share my deepest thoughts and feelings?* As these questions buzzed around in my head, something became crystal clear: I didn't need a bodyguard anymore. I had fought some hard battles and come out the other side stronger and self-assured. From the work I'd done over the past couple of years, I had learned to recognize safety, and *I* could set boundaries. I could be my own protector.

Walking along the wooden boardwalk toward the water, smelling the salty air, I witnessed something fantastic occurring in my internal world: the emotionally mature "wise adult" part of me, relating to the part of me that I'd held on to the longest: my "fearful survivalist" part. They were talking to each other—*listening* to each other—without me even trying.

In the past, if I'd felt afraid, my survival instincts would have kicked in and urgently pulled me out of the moment through fight, flight, fawn, or freeze. At an earlier time in my life, I may have noticed the boys, felt fear and jolted my hand away from Mae. But not this time. This time, when I felt the fear, I took the time to decide how to respond. I took a deep breath and squeezed Mae's hand tighter. I stayed true to me. I felt this shift in my cells and bones. It felt massive.

We reached the sand, and I kicked off my sandals—digging my feet in and feeling the warmth on my soles. *I could keep myself safe.*

I want a partner, my inner wise adult decided calmly and with authority. Someone with a wide-open heart and the courage to grow into something bigger with me. I wanted a person who would dig their hands in and work and didn't blame others when things got hard. Someone who could love me and my daughter with gentleness and strength. Mae made me feel secure emotionally—safe to be all aspects of me. It felt risky to lean into trusting someone new, but when we talked, I led with honesty. In the past, my vulnerability and softness had been used by others to hurt me, so sharing myself vulnerably with Mae required real courage. I was clear that I wanted to do dating and intimacy differently, and I was determined to show up as my realest self. Each time I opened up, Mae responded with more love and tender support. In the bedroom, I was free, encouraged even, to play with the parts of me that enjoyed power games: the winner, the villain, the slut, and the helpless damsel in distress. All parts of me were on display in this relationship and everything was met with enthusiastic acceptance. I hadn't known what I'd been missing, until now. My stomach softened. I leaned in and pulled Mae closer.

"Let's go sit over there for a little," I said, gesturing to an empty spot on the sand near Lifeguard Tower 26. The world slowed down, I leaned into my own knowing. I no longer needed a powerful guru, a controlling husband, or a pedigreed journalist to tell me what to do or who to be—I trusted my own ability to make the right decisions for me. And Mae was a right decision—I knew this with every part of me.

Watching the Santa Monica Ferris Wheel lights spin in the distance, I saw how far I'd come. And now I had someone extraordinary to walk with me.

"This feels great," Mae said and smiled at me, bending down to dig their hands in the warm sand then letting the grains slip through their fingers. A hallmark of healing is a less rigid, more flexible mind. A mind that can hold space for shades of gray. Falling in love with Mae had me twirling in silver sparkles, white smoke, and charcoal thunder clouds—heart beaming, face to the sky like I was a dancing whirling dervish.

But even with my head spinning with happiness, I knew myself—and I'd learned by now that my enthusiastic feelings could sometimes lead me astray. So early on in our relationship, I set up some tests for Mae. I needed to see how they would respond to certain things that were non-negotiable for me. I wanted to see how safe it was to keep allowing myself to fall in love with this person.

I told Mae about The Doctor and the email I'd sent him asking for kinkier sex. In their show *Feel Good*, Mae's character role-played some similar funny scenarios with their girlfriend, so I believed Mae would be up for that kind of play in the bedroom. Still, I didn't want to waste time. I needed to know explicitly and directly how they felt. I forwarded the email to see how Mae would react. An hour later I had a response.

Mae had written back in the voice of The Doctor, celebrating my courage and willingness to open up the space to talk about this topic in a "judgment-free zone." And when, a few days later, Mae sent a role-play script they'd written for us, I knew I'd met my match in the bedroom.

Not long after that, I introduced Mae to Ama, really hoping the two of them would hit it off. This was perhaps the biggest test. *What will I do if they don't like each other?* Ama had a Friday off school and my sister had planned a morning for us at a museum she liked downtown. I invited Mae to join us, and told Ama my friend was coming, too. When Mae arrived, Ama hid behind my leg and pulled me down to her level. "Mom, who's that guy?" she whispered in my ear.

"That's Mae," I said with a reassuring smile.

"I thought Mae was going to be a girl," she said.

Just then, Mae handed Ama a gift, a light that made stars and universes on the ceiling. "You can put this up in your room and it looks like the night sky," Mae said and smiled at Ama. My daughter opened her arms to receive the gift—and truly the rest of the day went seamlessly. Mae effortlessly chatted with Ama like they were old friends. In the museum, we took some pictures.

"I want to take one!" Ama grabbed my phone, somehow managing to snap a candid shot of me and Mae with a filter full of pink hearts. My girl, she knew.

"Can we have another playdate with Mae?" Ama asked me on the way home. My heart melted. I was safe to keep falling.

F. Scott Fitzgerald said, "The test of a first-rate intelligence is the ability to hold two opposed ideas in mind at the same time and still retain the ability to function." Being in a relationship with a nonbinary person completely exploded my brain. There was no way for me to categorize Mae and perform my typical behavior. In seeing and loving Mae for Mae—not as a man or a woman—I also found space to expand my definition of who *I* was. My whole world was widening alongside my heart.

In survival mode, our minds narrow to focus on the thing that will give us the best chance to stay alive. We begin to operate on "either/or"—becoming rigid in our mindset and fixated on categorizing things into good vs. bad, right vs. wrong, black vs. white, so that we can feel a sense of control and safety in an "unsafe" world. That's what I tended to do in relationships. I constricted myself into the role of "woman" so my "man" would feel strong and confident. I played smaller than I really was to stay safe, to be the one who did the rejecting, not the one who'd be dumped. But now that I was in a queer relationship, and fully committed to truth, the old binary survival structures I'd built my intimate relationships on dissolved like a fizzy bath bomb. It was beautifully simple—easy and sweet.

The benefits of all my therapeutic bodywork were starting to solidify along these lines, too. I was learning firsthand that healing your nervous system creates new access to different, more helpful thoughts. My thoughts now were warm, trusting, and future oriented. I felt settled inside my skin. With this kind of safety, I moved beyond limited survival thinking;

I expanded into my unlimited soul's perspective. I know my soul to be the "me" that lies beyond fear and judgment. A deeper part of me that is timeless and unafraid. The soul's goal is growth, and it sees everything as useful toward this end. All experiences, whether pleasurable or painful, can be soul food.

I was starting to learn that while survival mode may be either/or, the soul is nurtured by yes/and. I'd begun to embrace a new and powerful question: *What if everything—the good, the bad, the high, the low—was all okay?* The idea was liberating and neutralizing. It helped me when things were hard or upsetting. I stopped judging my emotions and started simply accepting them. *What if this uncomfortable feeling is okay?* I started to offer this question and shared personal stories with clients during my coaching sessions. I watched lightbulbs go off for them as they started to accept the past and release the power it held over them; they let go of self-blame or judgment about the things they did when they were in survival mode. They claimed the present moment just as it was, and when they sunk their teeth into it, they had miraculous shifts internally and externally—some were feeling more alive than ever, falling in love, getting promoted at work, selling their houses, or buying a house for the first time. Their courage, self-worth, and willingness to bet on themselves were soaring.

As a professional improv actor, Mae was already a pro at yes/and. It's a game they play in improv to help scenes flow. Someone introduces an idea, and the other actor says yes and adds something else. The scenes build from there, playing off one another's creativity and taking funny, dramatic twists and turns. It works well offstage too; when you say yes to what is occurring and you add your own creativity to the moment, you're bound to have more enjoyment and flow in your life.

After that moment on the beach, I kept saying yes to Mae. Over the following six months we built something together. We showed up for each other. We played together and went on adventures. We held each other's dreams and laughed at each other's silly quirks. Mae didn't make fun of me when I shared my passion for Fiona Apple and Whitney Houston like the last guy I'd gone out with. We created a shared nineties playlist on Spotify mashing up our favorite nostalgic music. We drank red wine at my small dining room table and read stories and talked about true and vulnerable things. I felt liberated—I was in a whole new world of truth and authenticity and real love. We cuddled up and visualized a bigger life together—a house with high ceilings and expansive views. A home and a family of our own.

11

Traitor

"**D**o you want to do *The Traitors?* We're casting season two of this murder-mystery reality competition show set in Scotland, and we think you'd be amazing. This cast is really special. We're very excited about this season, and we hope you'll join us."

In the pink glow cast by the neon LOVE sign in my living room, I reread the email from the casting director. My heart leaped. I *did* want to do it. A split second later, my stomach dropped. *But how could I?* For the past two years, I'd been digging deep into the archives of my personal history, practicing truth-telling and searing emotional honesty, and training my nervous system to seek peace and calm. I knew that playing *Traitors,* a game built on lying and emotional manipulation, would throw me back into the chaos of survival that I'd been actively and diligently healing from for years. I was nervous. But I was also curious— *Could I do it differently this time?*

I sat down on the armrest of my green couch. I knew so much more now. I wasn't the same girl who'd played *Survivor* all those times and returned home traumatized without a support system in place. I had so much knowledge about my body and my triggers. I had people in place who could help bring me back to myself if I came home out of sorts. Still, I wondered whether I had created *enough* capacity in my nervous system to go out there and play this game full-out. And after the game was over, could I recover in a healthy way? Could I return to the new peaceful, beautiful life I was building without a hitch? The opportunity felt like a personal challenge—a call to put all my new skills to the test.

A yoga teacher I'd worked with once told me, "When you want to learn something deeply, teach it." In that vein, I'd co-taught a six-week online course with my friend and somatic practitioner Kallie Klug called "How Villains Are Made." The program was a reclamation of the word "villain," a way to turn pain into power. I wanted to rebrand myself and the label I'd acquired so many years ago as something helpful and empowering. The course combined education about the nervous system, somatic practices, and coaching to help people-pleasers become more assertive, embody confidence, set clear boundaries, and ask for what they want. It was a hit with our students. As a result of the course, some people asked for and received promotions at work, others left their unfulfilling relationships. One student told us he no longer needed his afternoon coffee because he'd gained so much energy from letting go of worrying about what others thought of him.

The work that I had done for myself was working for me

and for others. I felt confident that I could play a game like *Traitors* without contorting or limiting myself with concerns of being liked. Through my own exquisite self-care, I had developed the sweetest friendship with myself. I sensed that even if I sucked at the game or if I experienced backlash or criticism from my actions on the show, I'd be okay. *I* had my back. No matter what.

Turned out, I wasn't alone. Mae also had my back. After I agreed to do the show, they organized a mafia night at their house, inviting friends over so I could practice playing the game. About fifteen of us made a circle in the living room, perched on Mae's blue velvet couch and brown leather chairs. A ripple of anxiety ran up my spine as Mae, our delightfully wicked host, instructed us to cover our eyes, before circling us many times and tapping three "mafia" members on the shoulder. The rest of us (me included) were townspeople in danger of being murdered at any moment. Our job as the innocent: debate and uncover the mafia before they killed us. Everyone took the game deadly serious, and the conversation was heated and lively. I wasn't selected as mafia in any of the three rounds we played, so I practiced spotting people's "tells." In *Survivor: Heroes vs. Villains,* I was great at sniffing out lies, but it had been over ten years since that time in my life. I needed to see how good I was at picking up on deception now. Mae's confidence in me and unwavering support bolstered my belief in myself. I rightly called out a few of the killers and felt solid in my detective skills. But I was still nervous about my own untested ability to lie and get away with it.

The day before I left for Scotland, Mae came over bearing bags full of thoughtful gifts for my journey: a DVD player with seasons one and two of *The Office,* a toiletries case packed with a jade face-roller and razor, tiny toothpastes, cooling gel masks to de-puff my eyes, packets of Liquid IV electrolytes, and a special "bag of gifts" Mae told me to wait to open until I'd arrived in Scotland. I cried, feeling so loved, thinking I was really going to miss Mae.

The following day, more tears streamed down my face as I hugged my sister and my daughter goodbye. I worried about leaving Ama, who'd only transitioned to kindergarten a couple months before, but my angelic sister was fully prepared to play auntie of the year with schedules, phone numbers, and prearranged playdates. The sight of them together eased my mind a bit. I tossed my big suitcase full of sparkly headbands, floor-length wool coats, and tartan skirts in the trunk of my Uber, climbed in, and waved like a soldier heading off to war. Internally I was breaking down, but outwardly I smiled confidently while I watched my loves standing on the sidewalk in the bright California sunshine. My car rounded the corner, and they were gone. I was off to Scotland.

Believing I could do the show was one thing, but actually walking through the experience was quite another. I knew the cast would be comprised of celebrities from other reality TV shows, but I wasn't sure exactly who I'd be playing with. When I exited the plane after my grueling twenty-four-hour trip, my stomach twisted in knots. I was about to walk into a whole new landscape—an entire castle, *literally,* of unknowns. And I was exhausted.

"Hello, Parvati! How was your flight?" Jay, a handsome redhead with a megawatt smile, was the wellness producer for the show, and he had come to greet me at the baggage claim in Inverness.

"I need some of your energy to rub off on me. I feel like death," I replied, struggling to keep my eyes open.

"No worries. We'll get you to your room quickly and you'll be in bed in no time," he assured me. "It is quite cold outside, so you may want to pull a coat out of your suitcase if you have one," he added. It felt nice to be taken care of by Jay. I pulled one of the heavy wool coats I brought out of my bag and we exited the airport into the darkness—the blustery winds of the Scottish Highlands whipping around us. I really was in a new world.

They brought me to a hotel for my temporary stay before the game began. It was run like a high-security prison, with PAs posted at every corner with earpieces and walkies, gripping their schedules tightly, ensuring contestants wouldn't run into one another. Inside my room, a tall, heavy-set security guard dressed in black conducted a thorough search of my suitcase. The three of us erupted in peals of laughter as he discovered the secret "bag of gifts" Mae had left me, pulling out a hot-pink vibrator, crystals, and ironic Polaroids of Mae in a bubble bath covered in rose petals. Then things got real when Jay confiscated my phone. "Get some rest. It all gets going tomorrow!" Jay smiled as he and the security guard left, the heavy door shutting behind them.

I was on my own now.

The room was eerily still without Jay and the security guard in it. I walked to the window; it was too dark to see anything. I spun around and paced back and forth from the window to the bed a few times. A jolt of electric nerves coursed through my body. I steadied myself with a deep breath. "You got this," I said. My own clear voice cut through the thick quiet.

All of the healing work I'd been doing had given me the ability to stabilize and calm myself. I'd developed nervous system resilience and expanded my window of tolerance for stress. This time, I could feel when I started moving into survival mode—a tight chest, shallow breathing, and racing mind would tell me I was on the edge of my stress threshold. I was attuned to my body enough that I could now notice these signs. Whenever this happened in my home environment, I'd respond by taking a break, pulling back, and coaching myself to seek signs of safety to help calm my nerves. But I wasn't at home in this room. I knew I had some reserves and solid skills to lean on, but I felt entirely alone—without any of my usual lifelines.

I was also terrified of the *Traitors* round table. Unlike *Survivor* where we voted people off in secret, the round table was face-to-face verbal combat. There would be nowhere to hide and no escaping. If you haven't seen the show, imagine *Clue* meets *Knives Out*. Twenty-one people arrive at a castle in Scotland. Three are chosen as Traitors and the rest are the Faithful. The Traitors secretly murder one Faithful each night. The Faithful can claim power by finding out who the Traitors are and banishing them at the round table. To win as a Faithful, you must banish all the Traitors. To win as a Traitor, you must make it to the end of the game undetected. I trusted my physical prowess and challenge skills, but the round table would be a different beast—virtually no anonymity, no secret escape routes. It was just me and my ability to respond in the moment and think my way to the next move—in real time. But it was too late to turn back—and I wouldn't have even if I could.

I knew what was required of me. I needed to take this hero's journey.

Traitors started with a bang. Our black Land Rover pulled up at the castle for day one, and my jaw dropped as I saw Sandra, my nemesis from *Survivor: Heroes vs. Villains,* step out of the car beside mine.

"We've got to stop meeting like this!" I said to her, feigning enthusiasm and forcing a smile. Thank *God* I knew how to fawn. I proceeded down to the garden with the rest of my castmates, saying hello and attempting to gather as much information about each of them as possible in my most easy-mannered way, oozing Southern belle charm. It was like a past version of myself had arrived. And then—

BOOM!

I screamed as a cannon blast broke up our garden party. Alan Cumming, our glamorous host, announced: "Enjoy the party while you're all still Faithfuls, because soon it will be time to select the Traitors!"

My stomach dropped. We were nearing the dreaded round table. After dinner and a bit more mingling with the other contestants, we organized ourselves in a single-file line and marched somberly to the war room. I took my seat next to Larsa Pippen, ex-wife of famed NBA player Scottie Pippen and a castmate on the *Real Housewives of Miami* Bravo series. *Damn. I'd barely spoken to her at all*, I thought. Kevin Kreider from *Bling Empire* on Netflix sat down on my left. Another person I hadn't connected with much. *Shoot, I've got to move faster with these connections.* My inner critic was already finding me lacking. Adrenaline coursed through me. I gripped the sides of my chair with my sweaty palms and pulled my body down onto the seat, willing my ass to stay put.

Production came through and blindfolded us, tight. My pearly headband dug into the sides of my ears. I prayed that they'd show us some mercy and make this part fast. An eerie song from *The Hunger Games* rang out around us in the dark.

Are you, are you, coming to the tree? Jennifer Lawrence sang.

Alan slowly circled the table—for what felt like one hundred, maybe two hundred times—before he tapped the chosen two Traitors. Then we were finally told to remove our blindfolds. "The Traitors have been chosen," Alan said with a flourish. "But they are not complete. Tonight, the Traitors will murder and recruit. Do try to get some sleep." He smirked and sauntered out of the room, leaving us all to sit in the paranoid silence.

"I heard a noise to my left," Larsa proclaimed loudly to everyone at the table, gesturing toward me. I jumped. By "hearing a noise," she was implying that Alan had tapped my shoulder, making me a Traitor. She was throwing a target right on my back. Fight mode, activated.

"No. He didn't touch me. That sounds like a deflection

from someone who's nervous," I shot back. "You're barking up the wrong tree. I'm telling you." The game was on, and it was moving at lightning speed. Thankfully, my survival skills ran deep, and now it was like one part of me hovered above the scene, watching as I moved through it all. I would not lose myself in this.

On day two, I was still getting my bearings and trying to create a strategy on the fly. Many people believed I was a Traitor, though I hadn't been tapped. I was relieved to be a Faithful—I wouldn't have the added pressure of lying constantly—but I worried that I had very little power from this position and could be murdered at any moment. How would I gain people's trust to avoid banishment and become someone the Traitors wanted to keep around? I puzzled about this in the Land Rover on the way to our first big challenge. I was sitting next to Janelle, an all-star from *Big Brother,* and MJ from the Bravo series *Shahs of Sunset,* with two-time *Survivor* winner Sandra in the front seat. Any one of them could be a Traitor. My brain felt divided into multiple parts. I'd need to watch what I said, and at the same time discern who I could trust enough to share real information. But I didn't have time for that now. I had to hop out of my Land Rover, pull on a wet suit, and throw myself into a frigid lake to prove my worth in this challenge. This was high-flying mental acrobatics.

On the morning of day three, I was called into a confession room before breakfast. *This is not good.* I froze, spying the letter on my chair, and then my heart sank. I'd been the first murder. I slumped into my seat, deflated, but trying to keep my head up. I opened the letter and read aloud:

Parvati,

You have been recruited by the Traitors.

What? I thought, convinced that I was seeing things. *Oh my God. I haven't been murdered. I'm a Traitor now.*

I cackled in relief. Adrenaline filled me with a *whoosh* and nearly lifted my body from the chair. I would need to ground myself and act normal. *Jesus.* I'm heading straight into bright lights and beady eyes in the breakfast room from here.

Acting normal was easy to say, but incredibly difficult to perform. Everything inside me was ringing like a fire alarm. I threw the door open to breakfast, beaming my brightest smile, hugging my teeth together to keep them from chattering from nerves. I felt like I was under a microscope: exposed and par-anoid. Everyone was staring at me. Or were they? I couldn't tell if I was seeing accurately. All my movements and words enlarged in my mind like I had a huge spotlight on me. My hand shook as I lifted the coffee pot.

Steady, girl, I coached myself. *Just get through this breakfast and then you can go to the bathroom and breathe.*

"Who do we think was killed?" I asked Janelle, willing my voice to sound relieved that I was alive and concerned—like a Faithful.

Afterward, I rushed to the bathroom and locked the door. Bracing myself on the sink, I breathed big, heavy sighs and shook off the intensity of breakfast. I didn't know being a Traitor would be this unsettling. I also didn't have much time to regroup. If I stayed in the bathroom too long, people would get suspicious. I had to go out into the castle and act like I had nothing to hide. I also had to pretend like I was hunting

Traitors—engaging in suspicion, painting targets on innocent people. *Yowza, this is dark,* I thought, suddenly realizing what my new role was asking of me. Once again, I felt alone, and I wished I knew who my fellow Traitors were. But I'd have to wait to meet my team in the Traitors' turret after tonight's round table—if I survived banishment.

That night, we had our second round table. I'd kept my mouth shut for the first one when Peppermint from *RuPaul's Drag Race* butted heads with John Bercow, British Parliament's speaker of the house—afraid of the attention speaking up would get me. I hadn't been a Traitor for the first round table, but my innocence hadn't done anything to calm my nerves. This time would be even more terrifying because the layers of mental gymnastics had just intensified in my new role. I was a Traitor now, playing the part of a Faithful, praying not to be discovered. In my family, direct confrontation was something to be avoided at all costs. Growing up, I learned that passive-aggressiveness and going with the flow were optimal strategies to stay safe and get my needs met. In this room, however, faced with my bold, outspoken fellow competitors, there was no way to escape direct conflict. I needed to speak confidently. It was a trial by fire.

After a highly dramatic round table, Maks, a former pro from *Dancing with the Stars* and a Faithful, was banished. I felt relieved I'd managed to survive another night. I wandered off to debrief with the others in the bar, where I feigned confusion about Maks and how wrong we all were about him. *Act like a Faithful.* My head reeled. One by one, we went to bed. But not me. I was pulled into another room and handed a green cloak.

"Pull the hood on and keep your head down so no one can see your face. We're going into the turret to meet your fellow Traitors," a producer instructed. I looked up at him in time to catch the twinkle in his eye. *Zing.* Electric nerves prickled my fingertips and toes. The cloak was heavy and huge. I wrapped it around my shoulders, fastened it at the neck, and pulled the large hood over my head. It swallowed my innocence like a serpent—and with it I felt myself claiming my role: a full-bodied, lying, manipulating, deceiving Traitor. *Villain mode activated.* I hadn't ever had the privilege of accepting my villain title before, it was always thrust on me by others. Saying yes to the invitation and putting the Traitor's cloak on myself felt like a powerful symbol of my sovereignty.

I stomped into the turret in my black combat boots, cloak sweeping behind me. My fellow Traitors were already in place. I stepped into their circle, filling the empty space they'd left in between them, and held my breath. Slowly, we all lifted our hoods, revealing . . . Dan! And *Phaedra!* My jaw unhinged and hit the floor. I'd had many conversations with both in the castle and I had no idea they were Traitors. They were doing a really good job.

"OH. MY. GOD!" I squealed.

The three of us giggled like witches in a coven, and then we got down to business. It was time to murder my first Faithful. When I finally got back to my room around three or four A.M., I let out a big sigh. I'd made it through the day. *A true miracle,* I thought. About four hours later, my alarm clock buzzed. It was time to do it all over again.

For the entire three weeks of competition, my nervous system was flipped on to fight, flight, freeze, fawn. On the outside, I looked calm and controlled, but inside my body was in full survival mode. I didn't have my typical coping supports—hikes, ocean swims, music, dance, hot baths—so I just let myself ride the adrenaline. *I'll recover once I get home,* I told myself. I gave myself permission to feel crazy. And you know what? It was okay.

Playing the villain on *Traitors* was very different from my experience on *Survivor.* On *Survivor,* I'd felt guilty lying to my allies and blindsiding them because I didn't have enough experience and wisdom to distinguish myself from my gameplay. But with *Traitors,* I'd done the work. I truly saw it as a game, and I could separate my real self from the role I was playing—kind of like an actor in a movie. It didn't matter what others thought of me because I knew myself at my core and *I liked myself.* I felt a mischievous glee in donning my sparkly headbands and crocodile boots for the day.

Rather than feeling ashamed of my gameplay, as I had in the past, I relished the power that came from having a juicy secret and knowing more than the Faithfuls. On top of that, I was having a blast in the turret, cracking up and plotting murders with my treacherous colleague Phaedra. I hadn't chosen to be a villain, but clearly the role was meant for me. When I said yes to the recruitment, I was fully up for the part. Before I left home, I told myself that if I was chosen as a Traitor, I would let myself go full-throttle bad guy for the entire experience, because I had a stable base—a safe home, a loving relationship, and a group of healers to return to once this was all over. It would be fine no matter what. *I* would be fine.

The most fun part came when the Traitors were tasked with poisoning someone in plain sight. As soon as I read the letter detailing our mission, I knew the challenge was mine to accomplish. As the new recruit, I wanted to prove my worth—and I wanted the glory. With the coolest head and steadiest hand, I sought out my victim. Time was tight and I needed to first find the poison chalice that was hidden on a bookshelf in the library, and then I needed someone to drink from it. But when I saw the chalice, I knew immediately that the task might prove trickier than I'd thought. Everyone already had their drinks, and their cups were made of beautiful, ornate glass. Mine looked, very obviously, *odd*. It was metal and heavily unpolished, looking like something straight out of medieval times.

My victim would have to be someone I had a good relationship with, someone who'd feel comfortable with me simply putting a glass of wine to their lips. *I have to kill one of my friends,* I suddenly realized, dismayed. I made laps around the castle, rusty goblet in hand—going in and out of every room, feeling out the scene. There was a party vibe in the kitchen. I walked in and joined in the banter.

"I'm going to find out who the Traitors are and I'm going to kill them!" shouted Ekin-Su, a bombshell from *Love Island UK*. She was having a raucous time. I found her standing next to Peter Weber from *The Bachelor*, while my fellow Traitor Dan sat on a barstool on the other side of her. I winked at Dan and snaked my way around the other Faithfuls to get closer to Ekin-Su.

"Cheers!" I said to her as I rose my glass to her lips.

"Cheers!" she said and took my poison chalice in her hands.

"You can take it," I said, nudging her to drink.

She smiled at me and took a big sip. "I love you," she said, pulling me in for a hug and smushing our cheeks together. "You could never be a Traitor."

I smiled to myself. *Still got it*.

"How do I know you're not a Traitor?" Peter, who'd risen in ranks to the leader of the Faithfuls on the show, had cornered me in the kitchen. Peter had galvanized most of the men in the game and they had begun taking a moral stance on being Faithfuls. I overheard many of them saying they'd rather die a Faithful than be a Traitor. I found this moralizing repulsive— we were playing a game called *Traitors* after all—and I wanted nothing more than to shake things up and eliminate King Peter of the Faithfuls. But he was onto me. I felt like a wounded wolf with my back against the wall. Trying to force a steady voice I returned the volley: "How do I know *you're* not a Traitor, Peter?" Not my best work, but it was the best I could do in the moment.

Even as I enjoyed settling into my old villainess cloak, there were aspects of the role that didn't wear as well on me as they used to. Lying, for one, didn't come easily anymore. Though my work with *Existential Kink* had prepared me to release any shame or guilty feelings about "being bad" for the game, my body was rejecting the misalignment with truth. My neck had a crick in it since the day I'd accepted the *Traitors* recruitment offer, and I was so full of electricity that I could barely eat. I'd sit down with a plate full of dinner and let it go cold while conspiring with the people in front of me. Meanwhile, another part of my brain was darting around wondering what the other groups of people were talking about in different rooms of the castle. Who are they putting up for banishment? If it's me—*and I'm sure it is*—what can I do to protect myself for one more night? My mind was constantly scanning for threats, and my body was wired, on high alert.

I needed my body to get on board if I was going to make it to the end of the game. Each night, when I returned to my room, I gave my body a pep talk. I put one hand on my heart and one hand on my belly. "I know you're telling me that lying is not safe," I'd say out loud so my body could hear me. "I am still going to lie because it is my job right now. After this game is over, I will go back to what we've been doing: truth-telling and emotional authenticity."

The on-staff therapist met with us contestants one-on-one throughout filming. Toward the end of my time in the game, I'd been under heavy fire by the Faithfuls for days. Any time I walked into a room, they'd turn toward me and interrogate and accuse me. I felt completely alone, and I was dead tired. "It seems you've gone into a bit of a freeze state," the therapist said, speaking my language.

"Yep." It resonated, though I wasn't sure what I could do about it.

"Maybe you could try releasing some emotion," she offered.

"I never let myself cry when I play these games. Everyone's lying and no one can be trusted, so I just wall up my heart and play hard," I said.

"You don't have to be vulnerable in the castle," she said. "But you could let it happen here with me."

I thought of Mae and the yes/and game. Why not try something new? I dropped my survivor armor and let her hug me. Her kindness melted some of the ice around my heart and tears sprang from my eyes. To my surprise, it felt good to cry. The following day I felt freer, and the tears didn't stop when I was in the castle. I tried using them on Peter as a new strategy, but it was too late. I was banished on episode eight.

Standing in the circle of truth, under the bright spotlight, all eyes on me, I made my exit speech: "I have spent the last two years of my life practicing truth-telling and emotional authenticity. And really aligning myself with truth and integrity. Coming out here I wanted to play a Faithful game, but I'm not . . . a Faithful, I'm a Traitor."

My body felt instantly relieved to share who I truly was and say something about the work I'd been doing for years. It was hard performing my Traitor role, and I wanted at least one moment before I left to let down my guard and show my real cards in that castle. The Circle of Truth and my moment of honesty felt like a cleansing. Afterward, I dropped the mask, smiling easily, grateful I could be myself again.

"Baby. You're home!!" Mae picked me up at LAX. They flashed me the biggest smile and wrapped me up in their arms. They felt like a puffy down comforter—cozy, safe, warm.

"I love you," I said. It wasn't the first time I'd said it, but after such a long and intense separation, it felt monumental.

Mae's eyes lit up. "I *love* you."

Zooming home in the car, we sat close to each other, holding hands. I felt elated to be back in L.A. with the bright blue sky and the tall palm trees. I couldn't wait to see my daughter. I looked at Mae and beamed, feeling shiny and happy. Life was really good. It took about two weeks for my nervous system to settle down and release the hypervigilance and thought loops from playing *Traitors*. I had strange dreams that I was competing in weird missions and people were constantly after me, trying to banish me. I also had a bit of trouble reentering social situations.

"I feel like a fish, and everyone else is a bear," I cried to Mae on the couch one morning after we'd attended a party together. "Is that because you feel like an outsider, and you think everyone else is cool and in on it?" Mae interpreted my strange symbolic speech. Mae knew I'd tried to be friendly and social with my cast mates, but they'd been threatened by me from the start. So, I'd played the full three weeks as an outcast. I had repressed so much emotion and stress during the game, and because my body hadn't released it yet, it held on like I was still under threat. I thought back to a specific moment in the turret: Phaedra was angry I'd gone after the *Housewives* at the round table. "No one likes you, Parvati," she'd fired directly to my face. Her remark sliced the air above my head. I refused to let it land and hurt me, but that didn't change the fact that most people in the castle didn't trust me. I'd had a hard time finding inroads to build relationships, and that emotional effort was clearly still lingering around me.

"Yeah. I feel vulnerable and awkward. Like when I was a weirdo kid in middle school," I responded. Mae squeezed me tight. "You're the most beautiful, coolest, smartest person. You'll be back to yourself soon," they reassured me.

I cannot overstate the therapeutic effect of Mae's presence and love. It was new for me to have someone take care of me like this, and it soothed me in a way I'd ached for each time I'd come home from playing *Survivor.* I'd only ever returned home to chaos. This was the first time I had come home to safety. And I knew how to recognize safety after all the work I'd done building toward it.

I relaxed into their arms and took a deep breath, filling my lungs, and exhaled with a sigh. "Thank you," I said.

I felt proud of myself. I'd proven that I was strong enough to go back into a public arena of survival and succeed. I had recovered my capacity to perform at a high level in a pressure-cooker situation, and I didn't have to live there all the time. I could go into survival mode—and I could also come out of it. I had nervous system flexibility, and I'd built a support system and coping strategies I could lean on when I needed help.

I could play a villain on TV and come home to a house full of love, kindness, and honesty and fill my cup.

———

The Traitors aired in January 2024 and became the top-rated reality show in the United States. Fans from every reality TV franchise tuned in to watch their favorite reality TV celebs sneak around the castle and battle it out at the round table. People made hilarious memes of my squinty face and parodies of conversations I'd had. The fan response knocked me off my feet. Rather than criticizing me for the mistakes I'd made or the persona I'd played, they were donning my signature sparkly, beaded headbands and impersonating me at watch parties. They were having a ball with the show and embracing the campy drama. Because I had a sense of humor about myself and I owned my messy choices, I was also having a blast watching the show. I'd played fast and loose, far from perfect, and only moderately strategic. I hadn't come close to winning, but none of that mattered.

I felt victorious.

EPILOGUE

You do not have to be good . . .
You only have to let the soft animal of your body
love what it loves.

—MARY OLIVER

"I feel like I've made a huge mess of everything. It's all so chaotic," I confessed to Sara like I was a naughty schoolgirl, and she was the priest who could absolve me of my sins. I was back on my somatic therapist's table, doing the hard work of attempting to feel my feelings and collect the information they were trying to share with me. Again.

"Well, nature is wild and messy, and you are nature. Nature creates through chaos, organizes, and then destroys. Then the cycle repeats over and over again. So, it seems to me that you *are* aligned with who you are." With that, Sara dropped the mic.

Truth. I could feel it. Held in my therapist's acceptance and care, my body softened. I'd just returned from filming another reality TV show called *Deal or No Deal Island* a few days before. The island was paradise. I'd played with a wide-open heart and made deep, soulful connections. Now back in my normal life, laden with responsibilities, I was reeling. The morning after our last day of filming, I jumped on a plane from Panama, arriving at LAX at midnight.

When my alarm sounded at seven A.M. the next morning I was confused. My brain thought I was still on the island being awoken by a producer for the day's challenge. "No!" I said out loud. "They can't make us go." When I opened my eyes, I took in the heavy wooden dresser in front of me, the sliding bathroom door to my right, my big green duvet cover. *Oh—I'm in my bedroom in L.A.* Suddenly, it hit me: It was Ama's first day of first grade. She'd been with her dad that weekend, so he had the honor of getting her to school. I was my own responsibility. I threw my body out of bed, got dressed quickly, and arrived just in time to give her a hug and take a few pictures of her outside her new classroom. Then I rushed back to my car to make it to my somatic therapy appointment. The pace of life was making me feel frantic. I needed to slow down, but I was already looking ahead toward my next show—I'd agreed to play *Survivor Australia v. The World,* an international all-stars version of *Survivor* produced for *Australian Survivor.* I had a few weeks to prepare before I'd have to leave again for this new game. Life was not chilling out anytime soon. But all my somatic work had made me a quantum magician when it came to time. I knew how to slow it down inside me even if outside was a hectic mess.

Lying on Sara's table was the first time I'd been still in over a month. I took a full, deep breath and let it out. Tears welled up in my eyes. *Release.* My belly softened.

"What's going on?" Sara asked, pulsing a finger into my right adrenal. I dropped my full attention into the rhythm of the pulse. Steady.

"I loved my time away, and I'm sad to be home. Mae's been away for months filming their new show and things are feeling disconnected. I've been so happy, and it's disorienting to feel so unsettled," I replied. It felt good to say these things out loud. In hearing my own truth, my body relaxed even more, and my thoughts slowed. I felt more spacious and free.

Life was changing—new routines, new opportunities, new constantly evolving truths. As I lay on Sara's table, the sensations in my body were guiding me toward those truths. Though things around me were uncertain, I felt in control of myself. I felt clear.

Suddenly it dawned on me: *I had built a home inside myself.* I was comfortable and safe inside my skin. I trusted myself and I could sit in the unknown without panic or fear. I was no longer a prisoner of my past or my unconscious survival adaptations. I'd grown through the most difficult circumstances: grief, divorce, heartbreaking loss. I'd learned PhD-level communication skills to navigate co-parenting and emotional regulation to support my daughter through massive change. I'd opened my heart to love and fallen hard. I'd courageously put myself back out into the world of reality television and I'd come out on top. All my recent success felt tethered to the work I'd done to get to know myself, feel my feelings, and claim my story.

If I had to write a new story or start again, I had the power and skills to do just that.

I breathed a sigh of relief. I knew what I was committed to. What mattered to me. I was anchored in my values and strong sense of self.

I know for certain now that I don't have to be good. I don't have to be nice. I don't have to be liked. I only have to continue to let the soft animal of my body love what it loves.

IN LOVING MEMORY OF THE BLACK WIDOW

She served me well, and now she's free.

2008–2025

ACKNOWLEDGMENTS

I could not have written this book without the support of my brilliant writing teacher Sarah Herrington, who worked with me weekly for over two years to help me find my voice and artfully craft this narrative.

Thank you to my editor Maya Millett at The Dial Press for her unwavering support, enthusiasm, and sensitivity where mine was lacking, and to my agent Monika Verma, who took a chance on a first-time author and encouraged me to swing big.

To my parents, who first showed me how to survive and continue to show up for me with acceptance and love no matter what. My sister, Sodashi, who remembers it all and fiercely has my back even when I'm being truly ridiculous. My daughter, Ama, who taught me how to love. And the countless friends, family members, healers, teachers, and antagonists who reflected pieces of me to myself until I could see clearly what I was made of.

This project was a labor of soul and the process itself brought me to an entirely new life. I'm beyond grateful for everyone who midwifed this book baby. My hope is that this story will move you toward a place of deep truth, love, and safety inside yourself.

RESURCES

SOUL SUPPORT FOR WHEN YOU NEED TO FEEL LESS ALONE

Women Who Run with the Wolves: Myths and Stories of the Wild Woman Archetype, Clarissa Pinkola Estés

Awakening the Soul: A Deep Response to a Troubled World, Michael Meade

TACTICAL SUPPORT FOR HEALING

Complex PTSD: From Surviving to Thriving, Pete Walker

Waking the Tiger: Healing Trauma, Peter A. Levine

The Body Keeps the Score: Brain, Mind and Body in the Healing of Trauma, Bessel van der Kolk, M.D.

Healing Beyond Pills and Potions: Core Principles for Helpers & Healers, Steven Bierman

BIFF: For CoParent Communication, Bill Eddy, LCSW, ESQ.; Annette T. Burns, JD; Kevin Chafin, LPC

COPING WITH LOSS AND CHANGE

Untamed, Glennon Doyle

The Grief Recovery Handbook, John W. James and Russell Friedman

H Is for Hawk, Helen McDonald

Bittersweet: How Sorry and Longing Make Us Whole, Susan Cain

RECLAIM YOUR POWER

Existential Kink: Unmask Your Shadow and Embrace Your Power, Carolyn Elliott, PhD

Pussy: A Reclamation, Regena Thomashauer

Good Chemistry: The Science of Connection, from Soul to Psychedelics, Julie Holland

ABOUT THE AUTHOR

PARVATI SHALLOW is a mother, winner and five-time competitor of the hit TV series *Survivor*, and breakout star of *The Traitors* on Peacock. She holds advanced certifications in yoga, meditation, and breathwork and is a passionate student of various healing and therapeutic modalities, including structural integration, Somatic Experiencing, acupuncture, nutrition, sound healing, hypnotherapy, IRF, IFS, and many more.

parvatishallow.com
Instagram: @pshallow
YouTube: youtube.com/c/ParvatiShallowOfficial

ABOUT THE TYPE

This book was set in Baskerville, a typeface designed by John Baskerville (1706–75), an amateur printer and typefounder, and cut for him by John Handy in 1750. The type became popular again when the Lanston Monotype Corporation of London revived the classic roman face in 1923. The Mergenthaler Linotype Company in England and the United States cut a version of Baskerville in 1931, making it one of the most widely used typefaces today.